Cricket Rebel

Cricket Rebel

John Snow

an autobiography

HAMLYN

London · New York · Sydney · Toronto

Dedication

For my parents
and Len Bates

Published by
The Hamlyn Publishing Group Limited
London · New York · Sydney · Toronto
Astronaut House, Feltham, Middlesex, England

ISBN 0 600 31932 6

Photoset, printed and bound in Great Britain by
R. J. Acford Ltd., Chichester, Sussex

Contents

Introduction

THE DATE was February 25, 1971. It was just before 3.15 on a hazy afternoon. The Boeing 707 jetliner wedged itself deeper into the blue Australian sky and Darwin had just disappeared below the starboard wing when the thought flashed through my mind for the first time that my life as a professional cricketer would never be the same again.

I was taking my last look at Australia after five bitter-sweet months; five of the toughest, most rewarding months of my life. The seventh and final Test was still painted in every agonising detail on my mind but was already nine days old. England's Ashes-winning feat was over, just another statistic among the welter of facts and figures that spawn enthusiastically on the game of cricket. The happiness of achievement remained, although the celebrations of the victory had finally ended.

The champagne-laced, beer-laden, hangover-inducing rejoicings of Sydney, where the final scenes had been played, had given way to the equally enjoyable round of Melbourne where I had spent a week of farewells. More drinks, this time strictly ice-cold Aussie beer, had been pressed into my hands in Darwin's airport by Australians who had become temporary "friends" united by the game. With the battle over and the Ashes decided, the Australians were ready with congratulations and slaps on the back.

No doubt these same people had been crying for my blood only a fortnight before as they sat drawn to their television sets watching the action relayed from Sydney. And not just my blood but that of Ray Illingworth, John Edrich, Peter Lever, Bob Willis and the rest of the pack too.

There had been only one team in it then: theirs. Australia are supported with a one-eyed fanaticism and devotion England rarely command in their own followers. Victory on the sporting field is the Aussie way of exporting their strength, power and guts. It proves their existence and growth to the English tucked away on the other side of the world. But their team had lost. The mood had changed. I was no longer one of the enemy. They like winners out there.

Now I was alone. The jet was crowded yet I felt apart from my fellow travellers. Hong Kong, Singapore and Bangkok were ahead, offering a brief break before the next English season. It was time for reflection. Yet 40,000 feet up and day-dreaming I was brought back to earth now and again by a sharp tingling message from the little finger on my right hand, telling me the joint was knitting where it had been smashed on the wooden picket fence which serves as the demarcation line between fours and sixes at the Sydney Oval.

Geoff Boycott had already returned to England a wounded hero – batsman supreme reduced to the role of spectator during England's crowning hour he had helped to make possible. He had been the victim of a rising delivery from Graham McKenzie on a wicked wicket three days before the last Test, during a one-day game which should never have been planned for such a crucial stage of the tour. It was a match cursed by the players.

The other veterans of the campaign were still engaged in action. The battleground had now switched from Australia to New Zealand for a mini, anti-climactic Test series before their journey was complete and their escape route open.

That was why I was alone. I had only my "log" book for company and it was in there that I wrote:

> 'Well, I suppose it's over now. Darwin away, and with it the last look of Australia 1970–71. My thoughts go back over it as they went forward to it on that train way back in October.
>
> 'Funny how right they turned out to be, funny how the wrinkles have been added – plastic surgery on a life – which is the same for everyone.
>
> 'For me, I suppose, in its way, it's a devil exorcised, something which has stuck in my life ever since I don't know when. I feel sad and yet happy, richer and yet poorer for a childhood dream come true.'

A dream nurtured in the Worcestershire countryside of my youth was over. The dream – or rather conviction – that some day I would play for England in Australia and contribute in some way towards bringing back the Ashes. The dream that held me in the game when it threatened to desert my life or I it – as happens with so many teenagers rich in promise and ability – when I had finished at school.

What now? I had achieved what I had set my heart on doing so many years before but my career was not complete. The limbs were still willing, the mind still reasonably fresh, the game still called. Yet a different game!

Until the end of the Australian tour I had used it fully to provide my life's blood. I had enjoyed it, been thrilled by it . . . and also left with a feeling of frustration and anger as I suffered the game's idiosyncracies, prejudices, shortcomings and shortsightedness.

Australia had emphasised the gulf between players and administrators. A gulf of which not only our side was aware, but their side as well. The players, in the main, were branded as rogues to be seen and not heard. Yet anybody who could have eavesdropped on any conversation between those players in the privacy of their hotel rooms could only come away impressed by their devotion to cricket, concern for it and desire to safeguard its future.

It was the future which mainly occupied my thoughts flying out of Darwin and I realised that I could never stand aside again and not be counted.

I wasn't going to start a one-man revolution. Neither was I going to look for trouble. But I felt that from Australia onwards I was determined to have my say whenever the opportunity arose. I was sick of the biased attitude and incompetence which was apparent in cricket administration. In my opinion the game was suffering as a result.

Although involved, I was not so much concerned for myself but those coming behind me, hoping they would find a healthier, wealthier game. One with a secure future so that their dreams of playing for England in Australia had the greatest chance of being fulfilled.

During Ray Illingworth's reign as England captain, the lot of the professional cricketer had improved considerably. Yet I felt still more improvement was necessary if the game were to attract the players it needed and fulfil its role as a branch of the entertainment industry.

Now, in these turbulent post-Australia 1970–71 years of my career, I realise I have wrongly upset a number of people, even shocked and disappointed friends. I apologise. There are others I have offended by my actions and words. And I feel no remorse.

I hope the following pages will explain exactly why these things have happened to me and why I have taken the stand I have on occasions. I have been classed as a "rebel" and even a "misfit" by many people in authority. But not a rebel just for the hell of it. Not a misfit for the sake of being different.

To tell it properly, it is essential to go back to the beginning.

1941–51: Boyhood idylls and dreams

LIFE IS full of contrasts. Mine has been no exception. After a youth spent hawk-like wheeling and swooping on the innocent pleasures of the countryside, I suppose being free and eagle-proud in adulthood was the natural progression to which I could look forward. But pounding the same beat day after day, feet revisiting the tread of the previous day's labour and sweat? That was not part of the picture suggested by my introduction to life.

My parents told me I was an ugly baby when I first opened my lungs at the Nursery End under the sign of Libra on October 13, 1941. Nobody has told me I've changed since then. So much for Hans Christian Andersen's tale of the Ugly Duckling.

Earlier that month my parents had travelled down from Scotland to Worcestershire where my father was seeking a Living in the diocese of Worcester. This job initially did not materialise but in any case he had to return to finish his work in Alexandria. With my arrival imminent, my mother stayed with her parents in the village of Peopleton near Pershore where my grandfather was vicar. It was there that I was born.

Not a pretty sight perhaps but sufficient to send my grandfather cheerfully ringing up my father to report: "It's a young cricketer," to which he replied enthusiastically: "Good, let's hope he does well." No silver spoon for me, just a cricket bat handle to chew on. I understand I was not too impressed as I shortly went yellow with jaundice!

If wheels were already in motion to set me up as a cricketer, something else was also going on which would determine the course of my early life. Not long after I was born my father was offered and accepted a Living in Worcestershire which was to mean that I spent the first ten years of my life with the unspoilt countryside as my backyard. Huckleberry Finn could not have asked for more.

It was only a short distance to move from Peopleton where I was living to Elmley Castle, a beautiful old village nestling under the northern slope of Bredon Hill in the Vale of Evesham. The house we moved into stood in some three or four acres of its own ground next to the twelfth century church. It was huge. To a young child, fourteen rooms make a world of their own.

On the other side of the church stood the "Big House" of the village, an enormous place mysteriously veiled by trees, with its deer park running away up the slope of the hill behind, the rest of the houses paying homage at the bottom of its drive. A typical feudal arrangement was completed by the ruins of the Castle destroyed in the sixteenth century lying some way up the hill.

Here, young and in the heart of the country, I was oblivious of the fact there was a war going on. Happily the only thing I was told was the game of cricket and the only things that worried me were picking the bat up straight and watching the ball as my father threw it to me to hit. Innocence was bliss.

So my cricketing life was already being forged. Strictly by amateurs but amateurs nevertheless not without some qualifications. My mother's father had been cricket coach at Glenalmond and was still a fair player at the age of sixty, while my mother was a capable sportswoman at school. Equally, my father was an able cricketer, played football for Bo'ness and was attached to Queen of the South before going into the Church.

Not a tremendous sporting background perhaps when one thinks of Richard Hutton, Christopher Cowdrey, John Edrich, the Parks and Langridges of Sussex and many others in the worlds of cricket and football. But reasonable, and I'm sure I gained something physically from this environment.

Not everything though, for I believe that REAL ability is a gift that is either present or not at birth. It is difficult to define but there is no substitute for it whether it be in sport, art, music or what you will. Yet even REAL ability has to be worked on, for often an average performer who works can be better than a gifted one who doesn't. Ability is a basis for success, not a guarantee.

It is here that a sporting background can be most influential, and certainly was in my case, helping to develop any ability from the word go. Even so there are still many factors along the way which can change the course of things. Many a young person has not fulfilled early promise. But to that I would say: given ability, I believe if you want to do something deeply enough you will do it eventually.

Those are my thoughts now. I do not think they applied when I was three and just starting to learn about batting, unless family stubbornness was showing itself in my determination to hit the ball my father, with infinite patience, kept throwing at me. I suppose as I got older and succeeded in hitting the ball more often I enjoyed it more, and the game began to sink in its claws.

As time went by, the boundaries of my travels, as everyone's do, spread like ripples, but initially the garden seemed endless. We had just about everything in it – two ponds, a stream and waterfall, walnut trees, fruit trees, fruit bushes, large vegetable garden, pigs, chickens, even a bamboo thicket and our share of wild rabbits.

I used to spend hours wandering around, investigating, playing or simply lying in a strawberry patch or sitting up a fruit tree gorging myself and watching the day go by. Not every day was, of course, as idyllic as that. Schooldays forged new friendships and brought encouragement to cause mischief.

All the usual things came under our grubby hands – fishing, bird nesting, scrumping. A few unusual ones too like snake-hunting and trying to train young jackdaws. I became an avid tree-climber, once much to my grandmother's consternation when she found me perched 40 feet up a fir tree. I thought nothing of going higher, and not all this "squirreling" was useless, as my parents press-ganged me when it came to fruit-picking time, strapped a basket round my waist and told me to get on with it. Years later at college I learned that educationalists recommend tree-climbing as a natural form of physical education so maybe I was innocently benefiting all the time.

Being a boy I did my fair share of fighting to find an outlet for my aggressive streak. On one occasion in the school porch I caught my arch opponent with a beautiful punch. It ended the fight, but victory was far from complete and satisfactory for unfortunately my opponent went back through the door and landed at the headmaster's feet. I ended by losing out to the cane.

Like most boys I had the saving grace of an angelic side which showed when I sang in the church choir and trudged miles down snow-carpeted Christmas lanes to sing carols. I'll never forget the sight and smell when knocking on farmhouse doors which opened to reveal Dickensian scenes of tables groaning under the weight of seasonal goodies in front of log fires. Later I was prodded into trying to get a place in the choral school at King's College, Cambridge, though luckily without success. I doubt whether I would have played much cricket there.

Not all my official activities were as angelic as they might have been. One of my duties was to lead funeral processions from the church to the graveside before nipping back to toll the last bell. Had anybody opened the door to the belfry at those times they would have found an eight-year-old gleefully and furiously swinging Tarzan-like on the end of the bell rope.

Obviously not all of the time was spent with the boys or with my three sisters. Often I chose to be on my own, exploring, day-dreaming, thinking of the exotic places I'd heard about and, I suppose, developing a desire to travel. My father did not let me dream all my time away, for there was always plenty of work to be done in the garden. As I grew older I was given an axe to swing. Chopping down trees was excellent training for building muscles used when bowling, although bowling was still of secondary importance in my cricketing education at that stage.

The emphasis was still on batting and on *me* batting at that. I used to march out with the stumps, set them up on the large lawn adjacent to the house, take my guard and that would be the signal for another "Test" to begin. My father did the bowling, my mother and sisters did the fielding. Angela, being the youngest, always had to don Wellingtons and patrol the stream running through the garden, much to her annoyance. A patch of tall raspberry canes presented another natural hazard which necessitated jungle-like excursions by my other sisters Heather and Rosemary to retrieve the ball.

I never liked being out in these games and often, especially if I had scored well, selfishly argued with the decisions and even went to the extent of removing the stumps, bat and myself indoors. Naturally I was suitably punished and even collected scars for my shows of petulance. Once Rosemary hit me on the head with a watering can while another time Heather used the cricket ball for the same purpose.

These "Tests" were augmented by the real thing watched on television, which my father saved hard for so that he could follow his passionate interest. Overseas tours were followed equally avidly on the old "steam" radio in the lounge, crackling and hissing often to the extent of drowning the commentary but not our enthusiasm. My imagination knew no bounds and was further encouraged by a visit to the Worcester ground for the 1948 Australian game when Sir Donald Bradman, of course, scored his usual century.

I still have the tour brochure I got there. Strangely, however, all I remember about the visit is sitting at the New Road End and seeing this small figure walk out and walk back again, nothing of the goings on in between. All these things, together with the cricket books I read, left their mark on my ambition, and enlarged it, so that even at the age of seven or eight I knew deep down I wanted to play for England. More than that, I knew I *was* going to play for England.

So strong was my conviction I even went so far as to strike a bet with another boy of around my own age that I would make it. Remarkably the next time I saw that boy was some 13 years later when he was playing for Cambridge University and Gloucestershire and I was with Sussex. Tony Windows was his name, an all-rounder who was considered a good enough prospect himself to be taken on the England Under-23 tour of Pakistan in 1967.

His promise can be judged by naming some of those who accompanied him on that tour and later became full Test players. Alan Knott, for instance, Derek Underwood, Keith Fletcher, Dennis Amiss, Robin Hobbs, Pat Pocock, Geoff Arnold, Richard Hutton too. Plus David Brown who was already a full international. Unhappily, because of financial considerations, Tony decided to seek his living outside the game, so a place was wasted which could have been filled by another young batsman seeking experience.

At the time that bet was struck I had still to play my first game of cricket. This came towards the end of my time at Elmley Castle, though to say I actually played in a match is, perhaps, cheating. The only recollection I have is filling a gap in the field. But what memories I have of the games I watched.

Saturday morning, the sun rising in the sky, would find me hurrying away from the village, up the dusty path to the church, around the edge of the "Big House" pond and through the gate to the deer park. There the animals were shooed away, the wicket was pitched between the anthills, and then the game was ready to start. Ready to start but there was never a rush.

Those games were more social occasions than matches, and, in any case, batsmen were often delayed by some crisis down in the village or on one of the local farms. Everything was very relaxed and as friendly as it should be, even the team selection. It was widely known that one farmer kept his place because he provided milk for the teas though, of course, nobody ever mentioned it. In this way his feelings were never hurt and the milk supply didn't dry up.

The buffet lunches, prepared by wives and girl friends, were enough to test the strongest table and somebody usually managed to produce a couple of crates of beer or a small barrel of scrumpy cider from the boot of an ancient car to wash everything down.

After these lunches, sudden batting collapses, bad fielding mistakes or even dubious umpiring decisions seemed to multiply. One of the latter produced what must be a classic exchange of words between umpire and batsman which still sticks in the memory. Our umpire Cyril Eden, having slaked his thirst at lunch one day, gave a batsman out caught at the wicket soon after the resumption. Much perturbed, the batsman, muttering his way back to the pavilion, angrily demanded of Cyril: "What be I'm out for then?" to which Cyril replied in no uncertain terms: "You'm be out for the whole afternoon. That's what you'm out for!"

It was not unusual either for the odd player to take advantage of a hollow time – waiting to bat or after being out – to slip away and see what his luck was like with his snares. Many a rabbit left the General's park in a cricket bag when stumps were drawn, later to grace a local supper table.

Maybe I didn't play very much at that stage but, looking back, I don't think that was very important. Living in the countryside was more than ample compensation, for the freedom it allowed gave me the opportunity to develop skills like balance and throwing in the natural pursuit of climbing trees or skimming stones across a pond.

Yet not all my practice was natural. The art of batting is not easy to learn. I spent hours in our back garden trying to imitate Bradman's reported childhood practice of hitting a golf ball against a wall with a cricket stump. It doesn't seem to have done me much good, maybe because I cheated after a while and ended up using a tennis ball! Or was it because of the nearby barrel of scrumpy ever available to slake the thirst?

Not everything in this period was a success however. Maypole dancing provided another outlet for the "good" side of my activities, but I was once blamed for wrecking the traditional village ceremony. Each year a procession passed through the village with one of the local boys at its head carrying an oak branch and dressed in a costume similar to those worn in England 200 years ago.

Unfortunately, when it came to my turn to lead the procession, the oak branch was too heavy to hold in one hand in the normal manner. I was forced to use two during the march which meant I had no way of pushing back my hat as it gradually slipped further over my forehead and eyes with each step. I was walking "blind" as we approached the main village street and ended up marching down one side of the road while the rest of the procession kept to the scheduled route down the other.

There was one thing I regret now. My parents insisted on my having music lessons with one of my teachers, and these I suffered after school once or twice a week until I was beginning to play *Teddy Bear's Picnic*.

These lessons were akin to holding back the migrating bird and eventually one fine summer's day the inevitable happened. I refused to play, was rude to the school mistress and ran out to find the rest of the lads. For my sins my father gave me a hiding when I returned home, but that was the end of the piano lessons. My stubbornness took over and I solidly refused to go any more. My parents said I would regret it and they were right. I wish now I had persevered and ignored the call of the outside. Music is a great source of satisfaction, especially as a form of relaxation after a hard day in the field.

Still, as the ancient sages said, "that's water under the bridge." Nobody can have everything in life and I had my dreams. They had taken hold of me and, given the opportunity, they were going to drag me after them. All they needed was that opportunity. And that, happily, was to come.

1951-60: Schooldays. Junior Sussex sides

CHRIST'S HOSPITAL School, Horsham, provided my passport onward into cricket and also a complete change of life from those idyllic surroundings in Worcestershire. My parents initially wanted me to go away for schooling to the King's College Choir School, Cambridge. With my voice, that was like trying to get a crow into a canary cage. I also tried to get into King's College, Worcester, but I didn't like the dark, foreboding archway into the school, left my entrance examination paper a complete blank and only breathed freely again when I was well away from the place. I still laugh about it every time Sussex play in Worcestershire.

In between there was much letter writing going on and it was one of these letters fortuitously being in the right place at the right time that eventually led to my gaining a presentation at Christ's Hospital, through the Cooks Company and the Governorship of Sir Harold Kenyon.

Fate had dealt the opportunity for my dreams to continue leading the way in my life, which so far had not been a frustrating struggle against the odds. Mind you, I believe an easy start is paid for later.

The journey from Elmley Castle was an eye-opener across a continent and round a world of thoughts and feelings to the Prep School at "Housey" as the school was known. There, still wet behind nine-year-old ears, I was left in the hands of a second year prep boy, my "nursemaid", to be introduced to the way of life of a new boy or "squitt" as he was called.

A "nursemaid" was very necessary because of the complexity of the school and the natural trouble a stranger would have in learning its rules and regulations. He was also necessary when it came to getting into the famous "Bluecoat" uniform.

This was a considerable skill calling for deft fingers and a steady hand. We all spent nervous hours learning to put the "bands" around our necks. A two-inch safety pin had to be pushed through six thicknesses of semi-starched heavy material, avoiding fingers and larynx, so that one ended with the two bands tied round the neck something like a priest. Needless to say the "nursemaid" had to do that for the "squitt" for about the first week – just one of his tiresome jobs.

Wearing these bands, breeches, long yellow socks and black ankle length coat I certainly felt strange to begin with and conscious of the sight I presented when I was alone outside school. Together, however, we boys provided a rare and colourful sight even though I didn't appreciate this fact the first time I found myself in a group with the others. It was teatime shortly after my parents left.

Suddenly everything hit me as I realised my situation and the tears just poured out, so that my "nursemaid" was driven to despair and finally told me harshly to "belt up." Eventually I did yet the feeling of loneliness lasted the rest of the day.

I do not recall ever crying again because of homesickness. The reason was simple. The next day I discovered that we played games almost every afternoon. These attracted me like a magnet and pulled me headlong into the school life. During the winter it was a new game, rugby – then, in the summer, cricket, cricket and even more cricket.

I am glad I played rugby at school and into my early twenties, for it taught me to accept slight injuries, whilst being trampled on occasionally meant learning to get up and play on as if nothing had happened. I think some of this has carried over into my cricket and made itself useful.

Nothing, however, could knock cricket from the number one spot as far as I was concerned. I just didn't look at rugby in the same way and wasn't interested in the slightest in trying to play it professionally when a possible opening came later. I was conscious that an injury might curtail my cricket career, also my desire was to tour with MCC rather than to play rugby during the winters. It was hardly surprising I abruptly stopped playing the game when I was close to starting my Test career.

The coming of spring with the mowing of grass around the playing fields inspiring the thought of playing cricket was always a heart-stirring moment. An eager anticipation and excitement came at the end of the Easter term and lasted through the holidays until I got back to school again. An animal must feel like that when it comes out of hibernation. I still feel it today despite experiences calculated to dampen enthusiasm.

Throughout the summer most of my time in class was spent thinking about the afternoon nets or the game to be played against another Prep school and worrying in case it rained. I can remember various masters throwing things at me to try to bring my attention back from down some cricketing lane. Another irksome thing which was like a ball and chain around my enthusiasm was the compulsory lying down for half an hour after lunch every day. I would appreciate it now, but then it was like tipping itching powder over me and not allowing me to wash it off. When the bell sounded at the end of this session I would be off down to the nets like some caged greyhound suddenly released to chase the hare.

With other boys of a like mind this often led to chaos in the race to be first – and much scheming. If caught by a master in the rush the penalty was being sent to the back of the queue. The art was to make a calculated last-minute effort from just behind the leaders who would "spring" any possible traps by the masters.

There was a tremendous enthusiasm for practice and the goal of getting into the Prep side was, for me, an added stimulant. It meant something "socially" to be in the team, and this with my basic deep-seated desire for cricket and my competitive instinct encouraged me further on my way to success.

If I am grateful for the atmosphere in the Prep school which gave me a favourable introduction to playing cricket for the first time, then I am also grateful for the facilities provided for learning the game.

Don't tell me I was lucky. I know I was. It is a great asset to be able to practise and play on pitches where you learn to do things properly, whether batting or bowling. Suffering conditions where one ball goes straight along the ground and the next comes through head high or which prevent a bowler from putting his foot down properly does not help anybody. All the main wickets I played on at Christ's Hospital could have graced more than one county ground I've played on since.

But not all the "pitches" were refined. Much time was spent round the back of the House playing on asphalt with a tennis ball, old bat and a couple of dustbins for wickets. So long as I was playing the game I enjoyed it, regardless of where it was taking place.

Unfortunately cricket is a game where not everybody is active all the time and "hanging around" turns many a youngster away to a game in which he can participate more consistently. I know a lot of boys at school felt like this. To me it seemed a pity they could not share the fun of playing against the Parents team who had to bat and bowl the wrong way round. Or take revenge against the Masters, whose bats were cut down to a few inches wide and who could wear only one pad.

Not all the factors influencing my cricket at that stage were confined to the school grounds. My father still worked on me during the holidays but, more important than that, came another family move which was to account for the direction my cricket took in my teens. Shortly before I left Prep school my father decided he wanted a change and something more of a challenge than a country parish like Elmley Castle. So it was that we moved down to Bognor Regis late in 1952, when my father was appointed Vicar there.

At the time I was sad to be leaving the country but glad that school was now only 30 miles away from home, which had its advantages. In retrospect the move was ideal, for it meant I spent my childhood in the freedom of the country and my youth in a new world, a town. I am now able to appreciate both types of life. Also it left me on the doorstep of Sussex cricket when I was old enough to be able just to reach the handle of the door.

My leaving Prep school in the summer of the following year was accompanied by a heady note in the school magazine *The Blue* which read: "Congratulations to Snow on a very successful cricket season." This was accompanied later in the article with the names of three others and myself who "enjoyed themselves so much at Hertford (the girls' half of Christ's Hospital) that we wonder whether they might not be happier there." It must have been quite a farewell season. Oh that I could remember it in greater detail!

The move to the Upper School and the House of my choice, Thornton "B", meant that I started off again at the bottom of the hierarchy, a point that was soon made clear to me. The first evening resulted in me telling a monitor what he could do with himself when he gave me an order and my receiving a whacking with a squash racket handle which brought me back to earth.

According to reports, my rugby showed a great improvement in my first year, no doubt due to the fact that one of our housemasters was W.P.C. Davies, a blond giant with a remarkable turn of speed, who was then playing centre-threequarter for England. If he were refereeing a practice game and you had moved out of position, he would scoop you up under one arm and deposit you in the right place with a "there you are laddie."

On the other hand it seems my housemaster's feelings after my first season of cricket for Thornton were mixed. He recorded: "He shows considerable promise but he will never be first class unless he shows some enthusiasm and less offensive spirit on the field." Words that have been repeated since on more than one occasion.

During that year I came into contact with someone who played a part second only to my father in shaping what talent I possessed. He was the school coach, Len Bates. His father was groundsman at Edgbaston, and he was born in the groundsman's cottage, which is now the central part of the pavilion. You can't get much closer to cricket for a start than that and the game became his life.

He was attached to Warwickshire for 20 years during which time he scored almost 20,000 runs including 21 centuries. On his retirement in 1933 he decided to share his knowledge and love of cricket by becoming a coach. His devotion to the game is amply shown by his tale of how when he got home after the First World War he immediately discarded his rifle and went straight to the nets to practise.

From 1953 until the end of my time at Housey my cricket was under his watchful eye, and I was interested to hear what he had to say about my ability at that time when I met him shortly before his death in 1971 at the age of 73.

He told me: "I first saw you when the Under-14s came to the nets on a Friday afternoon, but Mr Gregory from the Prep school had already told me he thought you were a cricketer. You had natural ability and I thought originally you would be a fast bowler for you had long arms and legs and bowled "over the top."

"You couldn't help but be a bowler if you did as you were told but you were a bit stubborn. The rhythm was there, you could run up naturally with your eyes shut, you loved bowling and had plenty of stamina. You were a good natural bat as well, though often your batting and fielding looked lackadaisical, as indeed did your bowling because you moved so easily. You also made me angry because you walked back so slowly to begin your run, but there was not much else because you were so keen to learn and play."

A smallish, slight man with an experience-lined, brown, hawkish face, Len could read you like a book and, with a mixture of patience and philosophy, get you to do what was best for yourself. For instance, after trying unsuccessfully to get me to cut down my then outlandishly long run-up he once at practice put up a backing net to cut off the straight drives. This had the effect of cutting my run down by more than a third which brought complaints from me. Len said nothing, just left me to get on with it and adjust. I got the message.

Perhaps more than anything he instilled in his lads the desire to get better, think about what they were doing and have quiet confidence in their own ability to do it. He was always talking to me about what I was doing and explaining things to do with grips, positioning of the feet when bowling, different types of bowlers, batsmen and so on. In many respects I was almost a professional when I left school so good was his coaching. Money could never repay him in my book.

If I was making progress on the sporting fields I suppose I had to be slipping elsewhere, and that could only be in the classroom. My reports in this sphere suggest the tortoise rather than the hare. Looking back I suppose there must have been glimmers of hope. I can remember at one stage producing a whole series of doodles of rear-engined racing cars that now look remarkably like the present day models.

I also lost a little character-wise it would seem. I had not quite got Len's quiet confidence mastered. As a result I was left out of the colts rugby side for making too much noise on the pitch and telling everyone else what to do. As the games master pointed out, one captain and one pack leader are ample for any side.

On another occasion I was called before my housemaster for being big-headed about my cricket. These warnings I noted and became suitably less vociferous, which gave people the impression that I was just plain arrogant instead!

In the meantime, away from school, we had settled into life at Bognor, where my father joined the local Bognor Cricket Club and turned out fairly regularly. Naturally I soon became involved during the spring and summer holidays and gained a lot of useful experience on their Nyewood Lane ground. Those memories are slow to fade from the mind.

I can remember well one game against the West Indian side Antilles, who had playing for them, amongst others, the legendary Sir Frank Worrell. I had the honour – for that is what I deemed it at the time – of being bowled by Sir Frank and can see it all happening as if it were taking place right now so much did I stand in awe. Sadly my next association with Sir Frank could only be at a tribute by his graveside with other members of the MCC party touring the West Indies in 1968.

Before this game I made my mark with Bognor colts playing on a local prep school ground. Somehow I managed to hit a six over some trees on one side of the ground and was later told that only two other boys had done it in living memory. I was keeping good company. The two other boys turned out to be Peter May and David Sheppard, who both spent some time in Bognor when they were young. That record is one that will stand for all time for shortly after my six-hitting effort the school was sold and the ground used for building.

Another game I recall was against the Bognor club in a friendly when I turned out with my father for a church side. The details are hazy apart from the efforts of the Snow family in helping to hold out for an inglorious draw.

We batted second and soon faced a hopeless target when we lost our first four wickets for 33 runs. That was the time for me to make my entry as a 13-year-old still dreaming in those days of a career as England's premier batsman. Survival, eating away the minutes that remained, was just as important as runs and I managed to hold out until shortly before the close. By that time I had become second top scorer with 33 runs in taking the score to 106 for eight. Top scorer? My father with an unbeaten 66 not out, having led the way in a 40-run partnership with me. One day at least when others were grateful for the stubbornness of the Snows.

It was clear that if I were to develop and get the opportunity of playing top class cricket it had to come through a county club, so my father arranged for me to attend the Easter coaching nets which Sussex organised at Middleton-on-Sea, about three miles from Bognor. From this seed my connections with Sussex and my career grew.

There and back four times a day for morning and afternoon net sessions meant a 12-mile cycle ride but it was well worth it. I was placed under the guidance of Sussex players Don Bates and Ken Suttle, the latter a bouncy little man and a glutton for any kind of sporting activity. He was a very capable footballer as well as a cricketer, but not, it appeared, a very good fortune teller.

As a result of that Easter coaching session he recommended me to the county as a batsman saying that I was a magnificent hitter of the ball and would possibly make the grade. My bowling he referred to as very erratic and not very hopeful, something I was to remind him about time and again when I later played with him in the Sussex side, opening the bowling and batting mainly at ten or eleven.

In fairness to Ken I still counted myself as a batsman at that stage of my life. My bowling *was* erratic, while I wielded a "Harrow" sized bat which had only to connect to send the ball far. Consequently I managed to get one or two balls over the club house, one or two more to dislodge tiles on its roof and, as a *pièce de résistance*, one through the secretary's window. Incidentally the bat had been given to me over the garden fence by a kindly neighbour, Mr. Knight.

This easing into the Sussex atmosphere was furthered later by attending indoor nets at Hove during the winter and the Easter coaching sessions at the county headquarters, which are still held today. Only now I'm handing out the advice instead of taking it.

I don't know how many more times in these pages I shall say I was lucky but I say it again without any apologies. It must be obvious that my father played a vital part in starting me off in cricket but it didn't end there.

Until I was old enough to be able to organise things for myself my cricket was firmly on the lines he laid down and he encouraged me in every way, perhaps even to the extent of overdoing it at times. He not only encouraged me but helped to provide the opportunity for me to play. The nets I have already mentioned. Then there was equipment, placing me in matches early in my career and so many other things. He enjoyed doing it and I have a certain feeling he was easing me along a path he himself would have loved to have trodden but that doesn't depreciate my debt of gratitude.

It is a debt I owe to many people who allowed me to use nets or play in sides, who merely accepted me or provided words of congratulations or encouragement here and there. They all helped to make things a bit easier. They still do.

Having said that, all the help and encouragement in the world is wasted unless the mental attitude is correct. That, at all times, is of great importance and perhaps gets more so the higher the standard becomes. Underneath everything, the will and determination must be there to provide a firm basis for development, otherwise everthing collapses.

That all sounds very learned and I can see it all very clearly now. When I try to return to my youth the picture often gets cloudy but I remember, even in the moments of doubt, about the only one thing I really wanted to do was to play cricket for England. As I grew older the more certain I became that I was going to achieve this aim. It was like having something inside me that grew and grew with time – a fifteen-year pregnancy.

Considering it now, I put in a tremendous amount of work on cricket between the ages of twelve and eighteen yet, remembering, it never seemed like work at the time for I was doing what I wanted to do and getting a world of enjoyment from it.

At school I progressed straight from the colts to the first eleven, following in the footsteps of Dennis Silk and Geoff Smith who later played for Kent. That meant school matches every Wednesday and Saturday, two hours of nets Monday, Tuesday and Thursday. Friday, unfortunately, was taken up by Cadet Snow having to make an appearance in the school Army Corps. Not very successfully I might add. I recall one brilliant attack on the enemy positions taking two hours of painstaking camouflage and stalking culminating in a devastating charge, only to find out the "enemy", fed up with waiting, had gone home 30 minutes earlier.

During the summer holidays I played an increasing number of games for an increasing number of clubs, gathering experience all the time. Some were adult sides, others schoolboy teams, but there was always something to gain from them. It meant that I had to forgo some opportunities to travel abroad that I would have loved to have taken but I felt I would make up for them on a larger scale later in life.

Towards the end of my years at Christ's Hospital I began to wriggle my way into Sussex sides through the Junior Martletts and Young Amateurs, who had connections with the county organisation and played a number of games on the Hove ground. At times the atmosphere was rather strained because most of the boys in these teams went to public schools and the professionals at county grounds we visited were often suspicious and far from complimentary. The Martlets and Young Amateurs, however, contained some very capable players.

By then I was beginning to consider myself more of a bowler than a batsman, due to circumstances mainly outside my control. Most boys wanted to bat and because I could do both I usually found myself caught up with a ball in my hand due to the law of supply and demand. As a result my batting suffered and I ended up being classified as a bowler during my early games with Sussex.

It was in this period that for the only time in my career I can definitely say I scared a batsman out. During a game against a visiting Dutch side a young boy came out to bat at number eleven. Unfortunately my first ball was a little short, reared up and caught him on the head whereupon he dropped his bat and fled back to the dressing room. We all stood around waiting for him to reappear but no amount of persuasion by his captain and rest of the team was going to tempt him back to the middle. After five minutes the umpires ended the game. Happily he was uninjured – just shaken.

I was by no means Tysonic in those days but I had my moments, particularly when playing for Bognor. On one occasion I bowled a batsman and a bail flew off catching the wicketkeeper, standing back, right between the eyes while the ball went over the slips and disappeared through the pavilion door.

On another, against Guy's Hospital, their captain came out and demanded that I be taken off before I seriously injured one of his players.

Another incident was perhaps more revealing than those in the development of my bowling and character. Having bowled a short ball at a batsman during one match he sarcastically patted the pitch almost in front of my feet. This is the proverbial red flag to a fast bowler.

The next ball hit him on the chin and he was carried off. Not very sporting maybe and even one of our own players complained. But I was not going to have anyone take the mickey out of me. Hitting him was an accident. The short ball was not. It was unfortunate that he got hurt in the process.

1961–65: Sussex debut. "Lord" Ted Dexter

When Wilf Wooller talks you listen. You may not always want to but that's a different matter. Big, bluff and powerful, he made his name on the rugby field as a thrusting, hard running threequarter for Wales as well on the cricket field as a Glamorgan all-rounder. Wooller is a man with strong views who thinks in black and white and adds colour with his language. They say they sent the mould from Wales to Yorkshire and made Brian Close when Wilf was finished.

I had no other choice but to listen when I first met Wilf. He was Glamorgan secretary, I a nervous stranger in the Sussex side making my first-class debut at Cardiff, waiting to start the second day's play. Rain was threatening, some of the boys were on the outfield practising, others grabbing a last-minute cup of tea, and only a couple of us were in the dressing room when Wilf put his head round the door.

"You shouldn't be playing lad," snapped Wilf looking directly at me. "I've been doing some checking this morning and you are not registered with Sussex." A friendly welcome to county championship cricket.

He didn't wait for an answer. I had nothing to say anyway. I was nineteen and I didn't argue in those days.

Wilf obviously thought I should not have been at Cardiff in that second week of August, 1961. As a matter of fact I thought the same, and I later discovered that Don Smith, standing in as captain for Ted Dexter who was away playing for England in the final Test against Australia, wasn't overcome with pleasure when he learned of my inclusion. Don had nothing against me personally. I just wasn't what he had asked for.

When taking everything into consideration – the Cardiff wicket, absence of Dexter and form of the other players with him – Don had asked Sussex for two extra batsmen to be sent to Cardiff. Instead he was flabbergasted to see second-team wicketkeeper Robin Walters and myself but no batsmen. That was my first experience of Sussex's organisational capabilities.

Personally I was surprised to be there because I wasn't even the most successful bowler in the Sussex second eleven. I had not played very often during the summer of 1961 and the few wickets I'd taken had cost me plenty. In comparison, Nick Treadaway, another young fast bowler with a good action and lively pace off the wicket, possessed far more impressive figures. He certainly deserved the opportunity ahead of me.

Nick complained to Squadron Leader Kingsford, the second eleven captain, when he heard of my selection and I agreed with him. I offered Nick my place but the Squadron Leader said that I must go.

It was quite a rush. We were playing in Essex on the East Coast when the message came through and it was not until the early hours of the morning that Robin and I arrived in Cardiff after trying to snatch some sleep on a train rolling through the night. The journey was hardly the right way for a youngster to prepare for his break into the big time, for that is where I found myself the following morning when Don told me I was in the final eleven.

I was late into the attack in the Glamorgan first innings, only given my chance when Ian Thomson and Bob Pountain tired after taking seven of the first eight wickets between them on a damp wicket which helped them seam the ball about. Jim Parks co-operated with a catch behind the wicket off J.B. Evans for me to claim my first victim, and Richard Langridge held another in the slips offered by Don Shepherd. I'd taken two for 12 and Glamorgan were all out for 95 in answer to our first innings of 270, in which Langridge scored a century.

Another century, this time by Alan Oakman in our second innings, left Glamorgan needing 373 to win which was well beyond their capabilities, despite a six-hitting spree by Jim Pressdee who was playing with a painful shoulder injury. He made 115, and hit one of his sixes off me, but I also had him caught round the corner, one of three wickets in the second innings. Five in the match. I was on my way. Slowly.

By the time I made this, my first-class bow, I'd left Christ's Hospital and moved on to Chichester High School seeking another "A" level pass before going to Culham Teachers Training College near Abingdon, Berkshire. I should have obtained that extra necessary "A" level pass at Christ's Hospital but, with all the cricket I was playing, something had to suffer.

Some of the cricket involved the Sussex second eleven in the summer holiday periods. The county had always had a reputation for playing amateurs and this obviously influenced my opportunities. It was a system which required very delicate handling if it was not to prove more disruptive than helpful in the long run to a supposedly professional organisation. As I have already mentioned professional players were always a little suspicious of amateurs. What was fun for one was a job for the other.

Initially, of course, these problems did not concern me. Indeed, as an outsider, I welcomed the system for my desire was to be good enough to play for the county and England as an amateur. In those days I pictured myself skimming off to Test matches and tours and then going on to something else in life. Young and keen as I was, I could see that cricket was only going to last for a part of my life and I should put down the foundations for the future in between playing the game. To be honest, I suppose I considered myself above being a professional.

Meanwhile cricket at Bognor was still playing a part in my life, and I appreciate now the help offered by Gary Cooper who captained the Sunday side. He guided me as often as he could, and encouraged me to control the direction of my bowling by gradually removing the number of fielders on the leg side, as I kept the ball on or just outside the off stump. He quickly took me off whenever I wasted the new ball.

It could not have been easy for him at times for he said I was not a welcome receiver of criticism. An opinion endorsed by the master of the first eleven at Christ's Hospital who wrote after my final term: "He has much natural ability and played a big part upon our cricket stage but if he seriously hopes to adorn a wider one the 'prima donna' temperament must be replaced by a more phlegmatic fighting spirit."

Be that as it may, there must have been something Sussex spotted in my approach which impressed them sufficiently to send me to Cardiff in that August, 1961. There was something in my bowling during that match, too, which encouraged them to give me another game that summer, this time at Worthing against Leicestershire.

I finished with only one wicket this time – a grand total of six in my first season – and also discovered the feeling that existed between amateurs and professionals. When I reported to the ground on the first morning I automatically made my way to the dressing room where the majority of the players were changing, only to be politely but firmly shown the door. I was with the professionals. My changing room was further along the pavilion. With the amateurs. We were not to meet up as a side until we got on to the square – each by our separate routes.

This outdated system had been brought in years before to divide the "gentlemen" from the workers. In those days initials before the name on the scorecard greatly outnumbered those behind the name.

By the time I entered county cricket, the professionals were beginning to gain proper respect and recognition. I would have been happy to share their dressing room but the professionals just would not have it. Reverse snobbery, if you like. Getting their own back. Silly? Perhaps, but understandable on the part of the older players who had suffered under the feudal system that existed in their earlier years.

With the amateurs or not, I was to make a mark against Leicestershire in my second match which was to stay with me for the next four seasons: my highest score in the first-class game. I managed to make 35 and was still unbeaten at the end of it. But on the other hand I discovered the harder side of a bowler's life. Cardiff had been an undemanding entry into first class cricket, but the match against Leicestershire was just the opposite.

Maurice Hallam, Leicestershire's opening batsman, made my batting contribution to the game look minute when he scored a double century and a century, both undefeated. Many of his runs came off me but before my confidence could be destroyed completely Don Smith demonstrated his compassion by replacing me with himself, saying: "There's a bit of stick flying around so I'll take it."

So my first "season" finished with six wickets. I was to advance that total by only another 30 during the summers of 1962 and 1963, my appearances limited by the need to qualify from the teachers training college and the regular availability and fitness of the Sussex bowlers. There was another reason, of course. The fact was that I was still learning the trade and lacked the control and discipline needed to keep going every day, Monday to Saturday, come cloud or sunshine in championship cricket.

I was learning other facts of cricketing life as well. Such as late nights followed by a hard day's labour do not go well together. It was a painful lesson, sparked off by a party which finished in the small hours of the morning as dawn was threatening to break over Brighton. My trouble was that Sussex were playing at Eastbourne and it must have been nearly eight o'clock before the sheets provided a welcome haven for my body, the soft pillow a very necessary resting place for my spinning head. There was time for two hours sleep before the resumption, again against Leicestershire. Possibly more, for it had rained quite steadily in Brighton during the night and nobody expected to get on the field at 11.30.

There was no escape. The rain had not been so heavy at Eastbourne, and the clouds were swept away as the dawn cleaned up the sky. The sun came out and we started on time, with me feeling a very sick man as Ted Dexter sent me down to field at third man. I can clearly remember the first time the ball came in my direction. Focusing was difficult until the ball was almost upon me, co-ordinating my movements equally so, and a sinking feeling accompanied the tumbling of the ball into my hands. Somehow I stayed on my two feet.

I was better the second time, at least in picking up the ball. Throwing it back was a different matter. I'd earned a little reputation for being fleet afoot with my loping gait and for having a useful arm both for speed and direction. That time my throw was high, slow and off course to the extent of bisecting the wickets.

Bowling was a strain when Ted called me into action, but it also provided a quick cure for a hangover. I soon sweated the drink and the late night out of my system and finished up with a couple of wickets. We also won the match by 124 runs to inspire thoughts of winning the championship title outright for the first time in the club's history. There were three home matches left in the season. Unfortunately we could do no better than draw those matches and finished fourth behind Yorkshire. Since then I've made sure the need for sleep in the life of a fast bowler has been respected.

I played in twelve matches that summer taking 29 wickets, and that fourth place in the table represents the nearest I have been to finishing on a championship-winning side in fifteen seasons of first-class cricket. I was also in on the birth of a new style of cricket that summer – the launching of the one-day cricketing bonanza in the shape of the Gillette Cup, a competition that was to change the shape and finances of the game. Sussex were the first of the new-style cricketing "kings."

Even today when this instant form of cricket provides county clubs with the means of balancing the accounts there are many who still frown on the development. Sussex have reason to be grateful for the innovation. Our success in the first two years represents the county's only tangible reward in nearly 140 years of effort – apart from finishing joint first in the championship more than a century ago.

I have every reason to be grateful too, for the final played out against Worcestershire before a full house at Lord's on that first Saturday of September, 1963 represented my breakthrough into the "big-time." In one way it was an embarrassing one.

I'd never been to Lord's before and had no idea how to get from the dressing room to the playing area. I was convinced it was from a door in the side – not through the famous Long Room – and wandered all over looking for this exit before being put right. It was a mistake Roger "Bluey" Marshall was to repeat ten years later when he went to Lord's for the first time when Sussex reached the final again in 1973.

From the moment I helped mop up the Worcestershire tail with three wickets for 13 runs as they were threatening our 168 all out, I became a regular in the Sussex side under Ted Dexter's command.

My spell at teacher training college had finished. I had to earn a living. The thought of playing as an amateur disappeared. John Snow, professional cricketer, was born.

Sussex, were, of course, ideally equipped for one-day cricket with their battery of medium-paced bowlers, even if the formation was accidental in its origin. We were stocked with medium-paced bowlers simply because Sussex had no top-class spin bowler on the staff. But more of that later.

In those first two winning years we had Ian Thomson, a master of line, length and control, who regularly took 100 wickets a season. Tony Buss, his opening partner, was far more dangerous to face than he might have looked from the ringside. Following them we had Don Bates, Lord Ted, and finally myself, all exponents of seam bowling.

Our attack varied little from one-day matches to three-day matches, which is why we were something of paper tigers when it came to the championship games. In Ted Dexter and Jim Parks we had two batsmen ideally suited in temperament and style to Gillette cricket who could build on the Oakman–Suttle opening platform.

Above all we had Dexter's captaincy. One-day cricket was his kind of game. It was instant and aggresive and its atmosphere brought out the best in him. He really became involved, more so than in county games. He even made a marked difference to our one-day performances when he returned for a season of Sunday League games in the early 1970s.

That 1963 season was my first under Ted's captaincy. Both my two games in 1961 and my only first-class appearance in 1962 had been when Ted was away on England duty and Don Smith had been in charge. When I came under Ted's influence for the first time I liked what I saw. Some people found him aloof. There was one member of the Sussex side who swore that Ted never spoke to him apart from giving him directions on the field. I'm sure this was not deliberate. Ted was a man of moods, often caught up in theories, keen when the action was hot, disinterested when the game was dull. Probably his moods were reflected in our performances. We would often charge around looking likely winners over the first day of a match but invariably fade. We had the basic equipment to succeed over one day, our weaknesses appeared when it came to the three-day game.

Ted was a big-time player, one who responded to atmosphere, liked action and enjoyed the chase and gamble. Maybe this was the reason he was drawn to horse racing; a dull day stalking the covers might be enlivened for him by thoughts of how his money was faring on the 3.15 at Ascot or Goodwood.

His interest in the four-legged creatures produced one or two hilarious moments and I can particularly recall one day in the field when the Derby was being run at Epsom.

With careful timing, Ted arranged for the drinks interval to be taken at the time the Derby was due to start and asked for a small portable radio to be smuggled on to the field, hidden under a towel. It proved to be one of the longest drinks intervals ever taken.

Everything went smoothly at the start. There were just a couple of minutes to the off when the two twelfth men appeared on the field, the horses lined up as we gathered round the radio. Then came the hold-up. The saddle slipped on one horse, the off was delayed while it was tightened so the drinks interval stretched and stretched as we waited and Ted listened to the race.

These days Ted is never far from his constant companion, a portable television set. He was the same then, and that resulted in one strange afternoon at Portsmouth. This time we were batting and Ted's innings had already been completed by the time the afternoon's racing was due to be screened.

The only trouble was that Ted found himself gazing at a muzzy picture when he switched on. For almost 15 minutes he turned, moved and juggled around the dressing room with the set until he found a clear picture – in the loo. And that's where we all spent the next two hours watching the racing, undoubtedly looking a little flushed when people discovered why we had been closeted together!

It was Ted who presented me with my county cap in 1964, but there was no real ceremony to mark my coming of age as a cricketer. Just a quick handshake, a word of congratulations and the cap plonked on the back of my head "Just William" style. Some members were annoyed and protested at the lack of formality but I had no complaints.

Personally I never had any problems with Ted because I never expected anything from him over and above direction, interesting conversation when he was in the mood and silence when his mind was elsewhere. Cricket wasn't the only thing in Ted's life. He needed some form of escape as I have always done. I could recognise this despite my immaturity so far as the first-class game was concerned.

We are alike in many ways and, as a result, I can remember only one occasion when we clashed on the field. It was a comparatively mild rebuke. One I chose to ignore and, fortunately, I got away with it.

The match was at Hastings against Northamptonshire. The rain-affected wicket was a little suspect all through and only stubborn innings by Graham Cooper and Ken Suttle, with half centuries each, took us to 216 in our first innings against some fine left-arm spin bowling from Malcolm Scott.

It was a wicket that called for the ball to be pitched up, allowing the conditions to do the rest, but I was still obsessed with pace and was trying to work up a reputation in those 1964 days. When Northants batted I dug one in a little short against Colin Milburn and it rose nicely for him to hook over square leg for four, causing our short legs to duck for cover. Ted was one of them, standing fairly close at leg slip, one of a huddle of close-in fielders.

His anger was immediate when he felt it safe to raise his head. "Why don't you pitch it up, you silly little bugger," he shouted down the wicket. Dexter or not, I didn't take too kindly to criticism like that.

The next ball was about the same length. Colin went for a repeat stroke but this ball rose a little higher than he expected, caught the shoulder of the bat and Ted took a simple catch. "Pitch it up like that d'you mean," I shouted down. Ted wasn't very happy but his anger deserted him as I followed with five more wickets, finishing with six for 39 in Northants' 85 all out. We went on to win the match by 99 runs despite being bundled out for 99 ourselves in the second innings.

The exchanges were far more friendly a year later when I made my Test debut against New Zealand at Lord's. Ted virtually talked me through the game.

For most of the time I was bowling, Ted was fielding at mid-on or mid-off and he kept up a constant stream of advice, hinting at the shortcomings and strong points of each New Zealand batsman, congratulating and encouraging me when I bowled a good one, offering sympathy when I beat a batsman without getting a touch, advising me and prompting me when I bowled the wrong line and bringing me back on course.

Unfortunately that was the beginning of the end of Ted's Test career, his brief flirtation with politics taking up more of his time that summer as he made his bid to become an MP. He was beginning to look for something more from his life, and cricket was poorer when it lost his affection.

Nothing illustrated that more than in 1968 when England were struggling against the Australians and Ted decided to make a brief comeback, offering himself for Test selection if needed. First he had to prove he could still do it after a long period out of the game. He produced no finer proof of his remarkable ability than when he strolled back into county cricket against Kent at Hastings and made 203, batting with confidence and timing against Derek Underwood on a turning wicket which made it appear he had never left the cricketing stage. Next day he was selected for the England side for the fourth Test match.

1965–66: Test debut and discard

KEN BARRINGTON and the England selectors rather stole the thunder of my Test debut. Although Ken would rather not have done. As I have previously mentioned, I made my entry into the Test arena at Lord's – nothing like starting at "headquarters" – against John Reid's New Zealanders in June, 1965, the first summer of twin tours to this country, with the South Africans due in the second half of the season.

In those days there was no John Player League cricket to compete with the announcement of a Test team which was always made around midday on the Sunday. Any young cricketer brought into the traditional twelve for his first Test outing could expect a back page headline in the national newspapers, with room for the usual "I'm over the moon" type of quote which seems to spill forever from the lips of sportsmen whenever they are asked how they feel, plus a potted history of past performances. As it turned out I was lucky to get a mention outside the bare announcement of the team.

That was all the "fault" of Ken Barrington, now a selector but then a whipping boy up for sentencing on that particular day. Ken's crime was taking seven and a quarter hours scoring 137 in the first innings during the opening Test of the series at Edgbaston, and his punishment was to be dropped from the England team after 57 matches. His innings almost brought the game to a standstill even if it did pave the way for Mike Smith's side to win by nine wickets. Peter Parfitt was brought in as Barrington's replacement and I was given the chance as the third fast bowler in support of Fred Trueman and Fred Rumsey, as Tom Cartwright was suffering from a stomach muscle injury.

So, after less than two full seasons' cricket, but the possessor of two Gillette Cup-winners medals, I was to win that bet I'd made so innocently years before with Tony Windows about playing for England. My place was gained largely as a result of taking 77 championship wickets during my first full summer in 1964 plus another 50 in the first two and a bit months of 1965.

This placed me ahead of my nearest young rivals David Brown

of Warwickshire and Jeff Jones of Glamorgan, but I was lucky too. None of England's fast bowlers had been particularly menacing during the first Test on a typically sluggish Edgbaston strip, and the selectors had apparently studied the merits and faults of fifteen fast bowlers – young, old, good and indifferent – before settling on their three for Lords, the two Freds being retained.

The Barrington story had hogged all the radio publicity on the Sunday and newspaper columns on the Monday, but nothing could disguise my pleasure or that of my father in Bognor who heard of my inclusion after conducting morning service. Maybe HE had something to do with it. I was in good company with team-mates Ted Dexter and Jim Parks also named in the side. I would be among friends as well as strangers when I walked into that Lord's dressing room.

That was a great moment for me. But it also turned out to be a sad one. My first Test match proved to be the last for Fred Trueman. A magnificent Test career resulting in more than 300 wickets was about to end, meaning I was to play only that one Test match with my schoolboy hero. About the time I was preparing to move on from prep school at Christ's Hospital, Fred Trueman was bursting on the scene in dramatic fashion, destroying the nervous Indian batsmen in 1952. He, along with Brian Statham, had served as my inspiration throughout my teenage strivings to copy their deeds. These two men I admired tremendously from afar watching them avidly on television, admiring their different skills as technicians backed by their desire to finish on top.

That summer of 1965 provided Brian Statham's last appearance in Test cricket too, when he made a dramatic return in the final Test at the Oval against the South Africans after being out of the reckoning for more than a season.

Unfortunately I was not to get a chance of playing Test cricket with him, a combination of injury plus the left-handed brutality of South Africa's Graeme Pollock settling my fate and leading up to the biggest disappointment of my career – missing the coming winter's tour to Australia.

I was satisfied with my efforts in that first Test against New Zealand, even if Mike Smith didn't call upon me until Freds Trueman and Rumsey had seen the shine off the new ball and Ted Dexter had been brought on as first change bowling into the wind. Once I got on, I didn't have long to wait for my first wicket. Big Fred Rumsey had shattered the early New Zealand batting with the new ball, his left-arm bowling taking the first four wickets at a personal cost of seven runs as New Zealand scrambled through the first 90 minutes to 28 for four. They lost two more wickets before lunch. Both to me.

Their captain John Reid was my first Test victim in my second over when he attempted a drive but succeeded only in snicking a catch to Jim Parks behind the stumps. My second wicket came on the stroke of lunchtime when I bowled wicket-keeper Artie Dick with a full toss. They were my only two in their first innings. Nothing spectacular.

I took another two wickets when they batted again, Artie Dick for a second time and Bruce Taylor, as England won by seven wickets to take the rubber with one Test to play. Again nothing remarkable but good enough, I thought, to earn me another crack in the final match of the series at Headingley a fortnight later. So did the selectors. But it was not to be.

When that first Test was over, the return of normality to my life came as a shock. Those few days at Lord's had seemed unreal. Somebody else had been bowling not me, for my legs had separated from my body and my mind had struggled in its own whirlpool. I suppose it is always like this when you dream about something for years and suddenly it happens.

Looking back I suppose I had been the last person to know of my selection. I'd been watching a benefit game at Ferring near Littlehampton, but had left before the news reached the ground. I later discovered this happens quite often as the names of the lucky ones are announced on the radio about a day before the official invitation arrives. One can understand the convenience of this to the powers that be but it is most unsatisfactory, especially when you are left out and the news is broken to you by strangers.

On that occasion it was only when I arrived back in Brighton that I heard of my selection from a Frenchman who told me that I was wanted for "a Test or something."

During the Monday and Tuesday before the match the butterflies in my stomach woke up so that by the Wednesday they were all moving quite well, especially when stirred up by talk of the game and the realisation that it was getting nearer.

When we reported for the pre-Test Wednesday afternoon nets Jim Parks and I were greeted by the others as we walked in through the dressing room door and the atmosphere was like that at the end of a school term, happily expectant. Having played more now, I think this is one of the most enjoyable parts of a Test for there is no disappointment, only excitement. At the time I felt lost as I tried to get out from under everyone's feet, found a place to change, then sat watching, listening and remembering the number of times I had seen Fred Trueman, Colin Cowdrey, Ted Dexter in televised Tests. I must have been about twelve when they first played – in another world.

I think I remember Fred Trueman showing fatherly concern and Mike Smith adding a few words of congratulations in his thoroughly open, absent-minded-professor sort of way. That helped to put me more at ease. Then there was the pleasure of all the best wishes arriving by post and the hilarity arising from the advice sent to others. It really is amazing what some people will write to suggest, like how to hold the ball or play certain bowlers; Ken Barrington, in a later Test, was even asked by one lady to stop "grabbing" himself when he batted as it distracted her! I've been advised to put more loop in my flight, put in a leg break and so on. Even told to have my hair cut. I suppose unconscious habits we have can be very annoying to viewers.

That first evening we had the real initiation ceremony so far as I was concerned, the team dinner. On the eve of every home Test the chairman and selectors officially welcome the squad at a dinner behind closed doors and you get the feeling of becoming part of a very select band. At the end of the meal the probable make-up of the team is announced and afterwards there is a general discussion of problems and points of interest. Not unnaturally this first time I sat there all ears; then, with the probability of playing, I left to spend a somewhat restless night thinking about the game and all its possibilities.

As it happened the following day was cloudy but dry, which meant the wicket remained firm, and Mike Smith told me I was to play with David Allen becoming twelfth man. The "spurs" – the England cap and sweaters – were brought up from under lock and key below and reverently handed over to me. They were mine. I knew what Eric Russell meant when on receiving his he said after the first ball had been bowled: "They can't take them away now old boy. It's W.E. Russell, Middlesex and England."

In the meantime Mike Smith had disappeared to toss with John Reid and returned to tell us we were in the field, which caused an immediate flurry of activity on my part and slight panic at the thought of being in the game so early.

The next half an hour was spent preparing for the game, in my case getting an ankle bandage and heel-pad on for protection and generally attending to small details to try to forget my nerves. Fred Trueman noticed my precautions and asked me about them and then, true to character, said he never bothered with that sort of thing.

If anybody were to ask me about my first ball I could not tell him anything except a vague feeling of having runs hit off me towards mid-wicket, although even that may not be correct. I do very much remember how I felt. It seemed my legs didn't want to work or hadn't got the message when my head had set-off on my run, leaving the in-between part holding the two together and me as a whole in danger of falling flat on my face. The ball in my right hand seemed totally irrelevant to my inner self, it was my subconscious which told me to hang on to it for I would need it – and so hang on to it with my sweaty palms I did. Had it been an orange I would have squeezed it dry.

The New Zealand innings ended around tea-time and now it was the turn of the batsmen to come under pressure. I, for my part, had a chance to sit and drink in the inner atmosphere of a Test at leisure and get to know some of the other players better by talking or watching and listening. Mostly the last for a lot of chat went on covering a wide field and much of it was humorous. Fred Trueman, for instance, with his encyclopaedic memory of past games and situations, would remark on something and launch off into "I remember . . ." with Peter Parfitt, David Allen and Fred Titmus acting as foils and prodders. Then somebody else would lead and the combination changed round. It was great fun and provided a broadening view of the game for a first-timer like me.

I was still very much a stranger. Of the other players I knew Ted Dexter and Jim Parks and how they reacted in the dressing room whilst waiting their turn to bat. Colin Cowdrey, Bob Barber, Fred Rumsey and Geoff Boycott, although joining in the fun, tended to be more studious. The last, at this stage, still had his "black" periods when getting out, during which he was best left well alone. Mike Smith, for his part, seemed to be riding the side with a loose rein, believing it knew where it was going and needed only an occasional tug to keep it on the right course. I think most players appreciated this and his openness as a person brought a better response on the field.

Unfortunately Mike is widely remembered in cricketing circles – especially when in partnership with his Warwickshire team-mate Alan Smith – as a very unreliable runner between wickets. Warwickshire tales of woe in this respect are numerous and I can remember a call between them in 1964 going something like "No A.C." – "Yes Mike" – "Wait A.C." – "Damn it Mike" – "Sorry A.C.".

Things I can clearly remember were my own concern for the batsmen to do well and my worry when we lost a couple of wickets quickly. I had forgotten this was a Test and we had a wealth of batting to come, and discovered I was very much against losing at this level.

When it was finally over I felt as though I were emerging from a cocoon. The side went its various ways and we were each left with a hangover of thoughts. So far as I was concerned the further I got away the greater the realisation and appreciation of what I had done became, and greater was the desire to have another go in the light of experience.

They say love is lovelier the second time around. I had to wait for my opportunity to find out.

I decided I might need some new boots for the Headingley Test and I began to break in a pair during the intervening county game at Eastbourne. Unfortunately the spikes were too long and stopped me so suddenly when I ran up to bowl that I tore muscles in my side which put me out of cricket for a fortnight.

When the side was chosen for the opening game against the South Africans at Lord's later in July I was still not fully in my stride which led to Warwickshire's David Brown gaining his first England cap.

He had been brought into the England twelve for the last Test against New Zealand and left out when the final choice was made, England going into that match with only two recognised opening bowlers. When a third was required for the first Test against South Africa, "Big Dave" was given his opportunity and took it well in picking up three wickets in each innings of a drawn game.

It was good enough for him to be kept in the team for the second Test at Trent Bridge until injury struck him down three days before the match. The wheel had turned full circle in the space of a month. My side injury had let in "Big Dave" after my Test debut. Now "Big Dave" was injured after his debut and I was to get my second chance. This see-saw of fortune has never ceased to fascinate me throughout my career.

As it turned out, it might have been better if I had stayed away. Graeme Pollock was the reason. When South Africa batted first and stumbled to 43 for four against the nagging accuracy of Tom Cartwright, Pollock suddenly cut loose to produce one of the greatest Test innings even that famous ground has witnessed. The cold statistics tell the story. He was just two hours 20 minutes at the crease during which he scored 125 of the 162 runs South Africa added in that period. A remarkable exhibition by a 21-year-old and one can only wonder what his standing might have been in Test cricket history if South African cricket had not been outlawed a few years later before Graeme had reached his peak.

The figures tell one story, but not the heartbreak of a young bowler trying to find a way to bowl to Pollock in that mood. It was a classic innings, full of rich strokes played mainly in front of the wicket with a perfectly straight bat, an object lesson for any schoolboy on how to drive with absolute assurance.

I was opening the bowling in that Test with David Larter of Northants. Unfortunately I felt the brutality of Pollock more than anybody, my one wicket in that innings costing 63 runs from my 22 overs. I did better the second time around taking three wickets but that did not save me from the firing squad when the team for the last Test was announced. Larter took five wickets and it did not spare him. Together we could not save England, South Africa winning by 94 runs.

So it was back to David Brown for the last Test at the Oval. Back to Statham, too, plus his Lancashire partner Ken Higgs who was winning his first cap. I'd had my chance of revenge and missed out when South Africa played Sussex at Hove in between those second and third Tests. South Africa made 391 on the first day, their highest total of the tour. There was just one century maker. Yes, you've guessed it. Graeme Pollock again. Warming up with his first half century in 70 minutes and dashing to his century with his second 50 taking only 35 minutes. My only consolation was that during that match I claimed my 100th wicket of the summer, the first time I was to pass such a mark in a season.

Despite that battering from Pollock at Trent Bridge and my failure to get any joy bowling against him a week later at Hove, I still thought I had a good chance of going to Australia with Mike Smith's team. Fred Trueman had left the Test scene, Brian Statham was too old to stand up to another winter of Australian wickets despite his successful return at the Oval, and Fred Rumsey had been discarded during the summer. The England selectors had to find a completely new attack from the younger brigade.

Four places were open, the traditional number set aside for fast or fast-medium bowlers in a touring party. David Brown was an obvious candidate for one place. Ken Higgs was a probability for another after his eight-wicket appearance at the Oval. That left two places open for David Larter, Jeff Jones – who had not played in a Test match at the time but, with the advantage of being a left-arm bowler, was obviously pressing his claims – and myself.

I was left out. And bitterly disappointed. Brown, Jones and Higgs I could accept but I thought I had a better claim than Larter who had toured Australia before and returned home with a poor record, the hard wickets affecting his legs. The same thing was to happen again.

We were playing Gloucestershire at Cheltenham when the party was announced. I'm afraid I lost my "cool", sending down a constant stream of bouncers the next day which took some doing on the third morning of a Cheltenham wicket at that time. They were not Gloucestershire batsmen at the other end of my sights that day but the England selectors. Appropriately enough I picked up five wickets before Gloucestershire declared and set John Mortimore and

David Allen against us to win the match handsomely. And they say hell hath no fury like a woman scorned!

Don Bates swears that during that day and the evening I walked around looking as if I were about to commit suicide, but I must admit from this distance that the selectors were probably wise in their choice. Once my anger had worked itself off I sat down and looked back over the season and over the criticism that had been made of my action. For all my 114 wickets that summer I realised I still had faults. I was not fast enough to be classed as a genuine quick bowler. I did not have the control one had come to expect after Brian Statham's reign. The reason was not hard to find. I was too chest on when I came to deliver.

As well as putting the brake on the pace I should have been able to generate through my run and rhythmic approach, this was also inhibiting me in another way. When bowling close to the wicket just a small amount of movement – swing through the air or cutting the ball off the wicket – can be sufficient to find the edge of the bat and induce a catch behind the stumps or to the waiting slip fielders. Bowling from a wider angle as I was doing requires a greater degree of movement to force the batsman into error.

That was my problem in 1965. After the disappointment of not going with Mike Smith's team to Australia I decided it was no use moping about it down in Sussex.

The Statham–Trueman era had gone. They had both been put out to grass in county championship cricket for the rest of their first-class careers. England was searching for a new fast bowling partnership. By their selection for the Australian tour, David Brown, David Larter, Jeff Jones and Ken Higgs were going to be given first crack. But I was determined I was going to be in there too. If I were, a winter at home was not going to do me any good.

The first reports were already coming back from Australia, stirring my desire for cricket in the sun. I made up my mind to search for ways of improving my bowling. One day I was sitting at home with nothing planned for the coming months and within 72 hours I'd booked my passage and was flying to South Africa in search of a game.

I had nothing arranged when I arrived in Johannesburg but within a few days I found myself playing for Southern Suburbs Club in the local league along with other English professional cricketers looking for a winter occupation in between the seasons at home.

Australia might still have beckoned when England's fast bowlers ran into trouble before the first Test started. With Larter and Brown injured, and Jeff Jones repeatedly falling foul of the umpire for running on the wicket, the MCC decided to send home for an additional bowler. Having just missed the plane in the first place, and playing cricket regularly in South Africa, I hoped they might have turned to me. Instead Barry Knight was dispatched in great haste. Australia was not for me that time but there was no great feeling of disappointment when I heard that Knight was going. The cricket I was playing was doing me good.

Playing cricket only at week-ends with the odd coaching sessions during the week gave me plenty of time to study my own problems and work out the answers. The wickets too, helped considerably. Hard and fast, offering a good return in the way of bounce, they encouraged me to adjust my approach to the wicket and my delivery action, so that I became a bowler of genuine pace.

By the time I returned to Sussex to prepare for the 1966 season I was very much more a "sideways-on" bowler, getting my left shoulder round more in the classic style and bowling from much nearer the stumps. All of this gave me far greater control so that I was able to keep the ball in and around the danger area of the batsman's off stump. And I had my surprise weapon, the fast leg-cutter which has always been my most rewarding delivery.

I had gained the extra pace necessary for me to be regarded as a strike bowler, one to be used in explosive spells searching for the breakthrough. I could no more be regarded as a stock bowler relying on line and length to keep the scoring in check and play on the patience of batsmen.

It was this change of classification which resulted in my first confrontation with the Sussex committee during that summer. The first but, by no means, the last.

1966–67: Troubles with Sussex. Test success

THE "NOOB" was the man who felt my angry blast. He had me on the carpet in front of the cricket committee at Sussex as a result of it.

The Nawab of Pataudi was his correct name then. He is now known as Mansur Ali Khan in scorebooks since his rank and titles have been stripped away by the Indian Government. He is the son of the Nawab of Pataudi who played cricket for both Oxford University and Worcestershire and captained the 1946 Indian touring side to England. The "Noob" also played for the University and captained India. He preferred to play his county cricket for Sussex after winning a blue in 1960 and was a superb player in his youth before he partially lost the sight of one eye in a motoring accident shortly before the University match in 1961. He was still a very good player afterwards; good enough to lead his country. A charming person, easy to get along with and a great practical joker.

I'd played with him many times before that clash of words in 1966 at Hove, linking up with him back in the late 1950s when we played together for Sussex Young Amateurs and the second eleven. It was then that I first came across his humorous nature. He had us all crowding round offering sympathy and asking for explanations when he turned up one morning for a match with various pieces of sticking plaster decorating his face.

He explained he had been returning to his hotel from a meal the previous evening when he was attacked by a gang who had cut him with razors. Several stitches had been needed when he was found and rushed to hospital and although he wasn't feeling very well, he was determined not to let the side down and insisted on playing.

Naturally we were all concerned. We fussed around him, treated him with every comfort and courtesy. Only when he had succeeded completely in fooling us all and earned our respect for the tremendous battle he had put up, did he rip aside the plaster to reveal an unblemished skin.

This, then, was the nature and the humour of the man with whom I had my showdown on the field at Hove. I have deliberately stressed my liking for him to show it was nothing personal. The summer of 1966 saw the "Noob", or "Tiger", in charge of the county having taken over the reins from Ted Dexter. It would have been the same whoever had been leading the side at that moment, for my frustration was directed at Sussex and what I felt were shortcomings of the cricket committee, not at the person charged with attempting to cover up those shortcomings on the field.

I cannot recall at this distance which side Sussex were playing, but that is not important. I do remember that the wicket was wet and slow after rain interference. And that I was almost on my knees having opened with the new ball and been kept on striving for a breakthrough.

All in all it had been a pretty lengthy, stamina-sapping spell on a completely unresponsive wicket before "Tiger" called a halt and took me off. I was looking forward to the rest in the wide open spaces of third man or long leg, needing the breather to regain my strength physically and to pull myself together mentally for another "onslaught" that I knew I would be called upon to produce later on. But no sooner had "Tiger" taken me off than he was calling for me to bowl again. That's when I exploded.

"Not me again. I shouldn't be bowling on this stuff. The spinners should be on," I told him.

"I agree," he answered. "But we haven't any spinners who can do it. You're the only bloke who is going to get them out."

"That's not my fault," I snapped back. "I cannot do everything. If you want a change, then you bowl the bloody thing." And with that I stalked back to the boundary.

"Tiger", of course, had no alternative but to report me to the secretary and committee when we left the field at the next interval. I don't blame him for that. He was the captain and responsible for maintaining discipline. In fact I welcomed the opportunity to meet the cricket committee, and explain my frustration at the lack of spinners in the Sussex side. I'm not sure that I got my message across but I certainly finished up being reprimanded for my behaviour.

For too long Sussex had played without top-class spinners. But more annoying was the impression that the county was making very little effort to find any and bring them on. They seemed quite happy in an all-seam attack, content in the knowledge that the Hove wicket generally favoured the quicker bowler and we could muddle through successfully with odds-and-ends spinners. I suppose we could cope reasonably well at Hove with five assorted seam bowlers in the side. But when we played on other wickets away from the county headquarters we struggled. More than half of our matches were played on grounds other than Hove.

For years critics have been complaining that spinners are a dying breed. People inside the game were lamenting their reduction in numbers ten years ago. At Sussex it seemed as though we considered their species had become extinct many years before.

When I came into the side Ron Bell, a left-arm spinner, was the only genuine tweaker of the ball on the staff. He was supported by Ken Suttle and Alan Oakman who both turned it a little in helpful conditions, but neither of them would claim to be a true all-rounder in the accepted sense of the word: equally proficient with bat or ball.

Only recently has the situation improved under the leadership of Tony Greig, helped by the insistence of the senior professionals that something should be done. In the last two seasons we have encouraged spinners Chris Waller and John Barclay, and Tony Buss has widened the search for youngsters since his appointment as club coach.

It is hoped, then, that the future will be better, but it is too late to save me those hours of frustration. In those days it was not good enough for the cricket committee to say there were not any spinners about. The county should have done much more, adopted a more positive and energetic approach and gone out to look for them.

I also question their selection policy in bringing youngsters to the ground for trials. From time to time they took young spinners on the staff, but none of them made it through the grades to hold down a regular place in the county side. If the original selection had been right, then a large percentage of players taken on the ground staff should have come through. Other county clubs still managed to find spin bowlers.

Earlier I commented that Sussex were paper tigers under Dexter, often threatening to win matches after the first two days but usually failing to press home the advantage on the third day. In fact we were always paper tigers whether under Dexter, Pataudi, Mike Griffith or Jim Parks. I put the main reason down to the fact that we did not have a good spinner in the side to take advantage of wickets breaking up on the third day. The number of times we were bowled out by spinners ourselves and were unable to get our own back and so lost the game are too many to recount.

As a result of this lack of balance much of the burden fell on my shoulders, especially in my earlier days. I was the rising young fast bowler, the strike bowler with Test experience, and was regarded as the main hope of bowling sides out. And the more Test matches I played, the more I was expected to succeed at a county level. There is a limit to what one man can do, whatever his job. That limit is reduced when overwork takes toll of a person physically as well as mentally.

It was often soul destroying. On wet wickets or slow ones, I was expected to charge up and down and let it go when I knew

I had no earthly chance of getting anything out of the wicket. This was even more frustrating when bowling to batsmen you knew you could get through time and again on a wicket with a bit of pace.

Quite often there was just no point in rushing in and letting the ball go at full pace only to see it pop up gently at the other end. This is the reason why I have been accused many times during my career of not trying at a county level. There have been occasions when I have not bowled at full stretch for Sussex – deliberately. I slowed down, concentrating on seaming the ball as the most effective method of attack on many of the wickets on which I have played. But immediately I slowed down or went off a shorter run people from the ringside automatically jumped to the conclusion that I was not trying, being awkward or snubbing the captain.

Fred Trueman has always been held up as a perfect example of a whole-hearted trier, but nobody will ever convince me that Fred bowled at top pace throughout his career. Even when he was recognised as England's leading bowler. There were countless times when Fred slowed down, concentrating on seam rather than pace, during his days with Yorkshire. Ray Illingworth has told me he often saw Fred boot the ball away with disgust when coming across a slow, bounceless wicket. Whatever his pace Fred, of course, always looked threatening because of his famous scowl, his theatrical gestures and belligerent attitude. I do not act the same way on the field, and have never been the showman.

Looking back on my own experiences I have been able to feel some sympathy for Andy Roberts of Hampshire over the last couple of seasons. In his first full championship season in 1974 Andy was overbowled consistently throughout the summer while Hampshire tried to retain the county title. I do not think he has ever been quite the same since.

Like Sussex, Hampshire have had their problems with spinners, being unable to find anybody to support left-arm slow bowler Peter Sainsbury. In the circumstances captain Richard Gilliat looked at Roberts as his match-winning bowler, the breakthrough man even when conditions did not suit him. The West Indian is still sharp, arguably the fastest in the world, but his average pace through the summer of 1975 must have been slower than in 1974. There is no doubt in my mind that Andy was overbowled by Hampshire, and suffered as a result. When including the four Test series Andy has bowled in since 1974 – a total of some 15 Tests, in India, Pakistan, Australia and in the Caribbean – it is not surprising that the West Indies were forced to give him a complete rest for three weeks before they came to England in 1976, because he had "broken down".

I am sure that Richard Gilliat would admit that he has been

forced to call upon Andy when he should not have been bowling, in the same way "Tiger" admitted he overbowled me when he wrote in his book "Tigers' Tail" (Stanley Paul, London, 1969):

> 'Ideally a bowler of John's tremendous pace should be used in short spells with adequate rests in between and he is usually more impressive and effective as a result. I knew this as well as he did but much as I wanted to help him, I had to be tough with John. Often I was forced to keep him bowling for lengthy spells because this was necessary for the team's success. Perhaps this did delay his choice as an England regular. But Sussex at that time did not have the overall strength to be able to nurse anyone and my idea has always been that the team's interest must always come before that of any individual.'

Certainly the first two Test matches in 1966 against the West Indies started without me, the selectors sticking to the bowlers who had drawn the series in Australia 1–1, although the captain changed between the two games. Colin Cowdrey took over again after Mike Smith's side had lost the opening game at Old Trafford on a wicket which made winning the toss vitally important. Unfortunately Mike lost it.

I was brought in for the third match of the series at Trent Bridge, taking over from Jeff Jones. Really I had left the selectors with little alternative after my performance a fortnight earlier when Sussex beat the West Indies inside two days on a green and well-grassed wicket at Hove – the touring side's first defeat of the summer.

So green was the wicket on that occasion that "Tiger" had no hesitation, when he won the toss, in asking Gary Sobers to bat, yet that was not the only factor influencing his decision. There were about 10,000 people at Hove that first morning and "Tiger" wanted to give them a chance of watching the West Indies bat. As it turned out the crowd was disappointed on that score, but perfectly satisfied otherwise in seeing the West Indies bowled out for 123. There was also a third reason for the captain's decision. On that wicket he was a little worried as to what a certain Charlie Griffith might be up to.

Fifty-six of those West Indies runs came from the bat of opener Joey Carew. Seymour Nurse and Basil Butcher were the only other batsmen to reach double figures, Sobers went for a duck, and I finished up with a career-best seven for 29 from my 17 overs.

Thanks to scores in the thirties by "Tiger" and Alan Oakman plus a fine unbeaten 64 by Peter Graves, we managed a 62-run first innings lead before putting the West Indies through the mill again. They made only 67 the second time around. I took four wickets to end with match figures of 11 for 47 and Sussex were left with a target of only six runs to win.

At the end of it not all the Sussex side were able to enjoy the taste of victory. Poor Ken Suttle for one. He'd been taken off to hospital for a jaw examination after being felled by a bouncer from Charlie Griffith, the first ball of the second innings.

It was obviously a delivery bowled in anger, a sign of his disappointment over the West Indies' batting performance, an attempt to show the Sussex "upstarts." Although we only needed six runs, a situation in which most captains would have used a non-bowler, Sobers set a very menacing field, inviting Griffith to show his paces. Charlie did not spurn the invitation. The bouncer thudded into Ken's jaw as he went to hook. Ken, ever gutsy, still had the time and presence to make a crack before he was taken off to hospital.

"He's not as quick as he was on the last tour," said Ken with his jaw rapidly doubling in size. "The last time he hit me before I had time to play my shot. This time he hit me after I'd finished it."

Whatever Griffith's speed, the injury and the situation he had created obviously worried Gary for he immediately took Griffith off after one over. There was still time, however, for Jim Parks to take a couple of bouncers. That over was about the quickest I've ever seen. Wicketkeeper Jackie Hendricks, standing some 20 yards back, was having to leap to take the ball with arms outstretched above his head. It was also "chucked." Griffith was in the process of re-modelling his action that summer, but this was a pure "throw-back."

He was also on target shortly afterwards. This time I had a grandstand view, from the other end of the wicket during the third Test at Trent Bridge when he sent down another wicked bouncer to dump Derek Underwood – making his Test debut – in a heap.

That was at the tail-end of a match as well. There was just Derek and myself, England's final pair, standing between West Indies and their second Test victory of the tour when Griffith hurled down the bouncer. The situation was not at all desperate from the West Indies viewpoint. There was no question of an England victory. We were more than 150 short when Derek joined me at the wicket. No question of rain threatening with a clear blue sky above. And no question of us holding out – although Derek had stayed 85 minutes in England's first innings in a record-breaking last wicket partnership with Basil D'Oliveira – for there must have been the best part of two hours playing time left.

Derek confessed afterwards that he didn't see the ball until it was rearing menacingly towards his head, growing larger with each passing fraction of a second. Instinctively he raised one hand and his glove partially deflected the ball to take off some of the pace before it caught him on the head. Down he went. I was one of the first to reach him and he was pretty dazed for some minutes afterwards. Pluckily he carried on but it wasn't long before Griffith bowled me to give West Indies victory by 139 runs. In my mind there was absolutely no excuse for bowling bouncers in a situation like that.

Basil Butcher had been the architect of the West Indies victory with an undefeated 209 in their second innings. My return read nought for 117. I got a ton-up in my next Test at Headingley as well. This time Gary Sobers (174) and Seymour Nurse (134) were mainly responsible in a sizzling 265 partnership in four hours. It was marvellous stroke-play for those watching from the boundary edge. Personally it was sickening having to bowl to them on the second afternoon, yet such was their command I could not help pausing to admire their ability. With the number of times the ball went to the boundary, there were plenty of pauses.

The West Indies didn't need a second innings. There was no chance for me to put a shine on my figures of three for 146. No time for me to redeem what reputation I had in the eyes of the selectors. I was out for the next match and England changed leaders once more.

When the selectors had finished their game of musical chairs Brian Close had taken over the hot seat from Colin Cowdrey, with the task of sewing together the tatters of an England side. Whether his was the influencing voice that led to my sacking I do not know. But sacked I was. Until fate stepped in and played a part again in the shaping of my career. I was preparing to spend some time on the beach at Brighton when John "Sport" Price, selected in my stead, cried off with an injury.

The match proved the turning point in my Test career as well as giving me the chance of gaining some measure of revenge for the indignities heaped on my bowling in the previous two matches. I was not to be dropped from the England side again on a pure question of form until the summer of 1973. Omitted, yes. As a disciplinary measure by both Colin Cowdrey and Ray Illingworth plus the mystery men in the background at Lord's. Left out, yes. But only on the grounds of fitness.

The result of Brian Close's first taste of Test leadership must be known to every student of the game. Victory by an innings and 34 runs to end the summer on a high note after an otherwise disappointing season.

Two particular passages during those four days at the Oval were to increase my standing as a Test player – both as a batsman and a bowler. The first came right at the end of England's first innings when Ken Higgs and I shared a last-wicket partnership of 128 in helping to take England to 527 and a lead of 259.

Tom Graveney had softened up the West Indies bowlers as only he could with an innings of 165. John Murray, recalled to the Test scene, frustrated them further with another century full of courage, and that left Ken and myself to do the rest. We were helped when Sobers made a tactical error.

He had spinners Lance Gibbs and David Holford bowling when we came together and although we played some nice meaty strokes against them, neither of us was completely secure. We played and missed fairly often but, worried that England's lead might grow out of reach, Gary turned to the new ball attack of Griffith and Wes Hall as his means of cutting us short. That was his tactical error. Immediately our problems eased. On that wicket the ball came straight through. To defend we both played down the line, sure of contact, waiting for the loose ball to punish. Then Gary returned to spin again and Ken gave a return catch to Holford.

We had set a new last wicket record for England against the West Indies, beating the D'Oliveira–Underwood effort two matches previously. We were two runs short of a record last-wicket partnership in all Tests, a record of which we were completely unaware. Just as we were completely unaware of the mass hysteria going on around us.

No Test match involving West Indian supporters can ever be quiet as they shout, dance and beat out a rhythm on cans, bottles, drums or anything they come across. Nothing silences them, yet the sound gradually faded from our ears as the partnership grew. We became totally immersed in concentrating on each delivery so that by the end the crowd and its noise might just as well have departed.

The most popular picture in the newspapers over the next two days was one of Ken and I sitting on the balcony outside the England dressing room sipping cups of tea. Thereby hangs another tale of the peculiar thinking of people in charge. The partnership was thirsty work and tea was the last thing we wanted at the end of the day. We each picked up a pint of beer and stepped out on to the balcony ready for the photographers. Before they could begin snapping one of the powers-that-be insisted we exchange beer mugs for tea cups for the photographic session. We musn't give the public the wrong image, old boy.

By the close of play on that Saturday the West Indies had lost four second innings wickets in scoring 135. It meant they started the Monday needing another 124 runs to make us bat again. A handy position for England but we didn't need the morning papers to tell us it was far from over. There was still Sobers to come, Sobers at his most magnificent, who had destroyed us repeatedly that summer scoring three Test centuries and a 94 in the first four tests and 81 in the first innings at the Oval.

Sobers' entry on that Monday morning was the start of another partnership which made the news the next day. A partnership between skipper Brian Close and myself. A short one this time. Just one ball in fact.

While Sobers was walking across the Oval turf to the crease Brian came up to me and asked me to give Gary a shortish delivery first ball. Not a real bouncer, but short enough for Gary to hook. Closey was sure Gary would accept the challenge whether it was his first ball or his hundredth. Brian was looking for the mis-hook, a catch somewhere in the outfield, and positioned two men for it just over halfway back to the boundary.

Doing as I was instructed – I *can* take orders – Gary went to hook and sure enough the catch was there for the taking. Not in the outfield but by Closey himself, amazingly only a couple of yards away at forward short leg. Gary was out first ball for a duck. The match was virtually over. Just the mopping up operations to complete before we left the field as unexpected heroes with a day and a half to spare.

Luck again, I suppose. Gary was only a fraction of an inch away from a perfect connection as he explained afterwards. "The ball from Snow bounced a bit but I suppose I was beaten by the speed more than anything. I didn't quite get hold of it properly, edged it into my body. It flew out to Brian and that was that."

Incidentally I was a few pounds better off for that unbeaten 59 in our first innings. After failing to score in the previous Test my father – still offering every ounce of encouragement he could – had offered me 50p (ten shillings in those days) for every run I scored at the Oval. A local Bognor bookmaker, hearing of the offer, topped it by offering my father's church funds £1 for every run I scored over 25. It cost them £29.50 and £34 respectively!

As I said earlier, from that Test onwards I was a regular member of the England side for a number of seasons. Twelve months earlier David Brown and Jeff Jones, both the same age as myself, had been considered England's spearhead with the medium pace of Ken Higgs in support. Thanks to that winter of study, fault-finding and rectification in South Africa, I had forced my way into their company, and that's how it stayed under Close's leadership during the following summer of 1967 against India and Pakistan.

However I did not finish the summer in the Test side. Playing against India at Egbaston I jarred my back low down and found that I was unable to bowl flat out without pain. As a result I was left with a constant ache which much treatment failed to soothe. By the end of July I was exhausted both mentally and physically by this, so much so that I eventually gave up trying to play and had some X-rays taken. Only then did I discover a sacroiliac joint abnormality. Although I was born with it, I was bluntly told it could mean the end to my bowling dreams. Naturally this was a hefty shock. There was nothing to do but go, fingers crossed, to Sussex County Hospital to have the joint stretched on a rack. Complete rest was the only cure for the inflammation. Fortunately the treatment worked, although, from time to time, it has been necessary to repeat it, notably before the penultimate Test in Adelaide during the 1970–71 tour of Australia.

Having settled this problem, I could only wait anxiously for the announcement of the names of the tour party to visit the West Indies that winter of 1967–68. The tour which saw the England captaincy turn full circle again, to be handed back to Colin Cowdrey after Brian Close had been found guilty of time-wasting incidents in preventing Warwickshire beating Yorkshire at Egbaston earlier in August. I was not too concerned who skippered the side at that time. My joy came from seeing my name in the 16-strong party, but I could not help thinking that Close's sacking was masterminded by people in the shadows at Lord's.

The selectors reportedly wanted Close to captain the tour party – on a majority verdict – but were overruled by the MCC committee who went for Cowdrey. It hardly seemed to me worthwhile appointing selectors if their decisions were not going to be acceptable. And did anybody imagine that such people as Doug Insole, now chairman of the Test and County Cricket Board, Peter May, Don Kenyon and Alec Bedser would send a leader to the West Indies whom they thought would act irresponsibly in any way? To me it was a prime example of one person having the "right" background and the other the "wrong". Something which has permeated the game since the early days of Players and Gentlemen.

1967–68: Caribbean experiences

THEY GO in pairs through cricket history: the fast men who in partnership have produced devastating striking forces to take their teams to the top of the international league. The list has grown in the 1970s by the addition of Dennis Lillee and Jeff Thomson who swept all before them in Australia's comeback as a cricketing power.

Before them Australia had McKenzie and Davidson, Miller and Lindwall, Gregory and McDonald as match-winning combinations. Hall and Griffith made a perfect partnership for the West Indies; Adcock and Heine, Peter Pollock and Procter for South Africa; Larwood and Voce, Trueman and Statham, Tyson and Statham for England. There have been other combinations too, but the ones I have listed above are sufficient to illustrate my point.

If I have been good enough–as some critics have kindly suggested–to rank amongst England's most successful fast bowlers, then people would struggle to pair me with anybody.

The truth is that I have never had a regular opening partner all the time I have been using the new ball for England. It has been like trying to dance a quickstep when the band insists on playing a waltz. I was lucky if I found myself with the same partner for two Tests running and I must admit it has been a big disappointment in my cricket life as well as providing an extra burden.

From Fred Rumsey back in 1965 through David Brown, Jeff Jones, Alan Ward, Peter Lever, Ken Shuttleworth, Bob Willis, Geoff Arnold and several others, I have hoped my partner of the moment would stay in the side and complement the work I was doing at the other end. The pulse quickened whenever a new name arose or somebody told me they had spotted a younger player with potential. However, for one reason or another, each new man failed to hold down a regular place.

I have not been alone in searching for another fast bowler. All England has joined in. There was a great buzz of excitement around the grounds late in the 1968 season when reports came from Derbyshire of the pace of Alan Ward. He became a regular in the Derbyshire side during the last half-a-dozen matches, and was the talk of the cricketing dinners that winter. I felt the excitement. When he continued to produce the speed the following summer he was rushed into the Test side and I looked forward to partnering him in Australia in 1970–71. Sadly it was not to be.

As I said earlier, the absence of a regular partner has affected me. I've wanted and needed somebody at the other end to share the striking role. Without that partner I felt extra pressure from the captain, my team-mates and the crowd, who have looked at me to provide the breakthrough, not only at the start of the innings but when the middle order batsmen looked like settling down or when the tail needed mopping up. The strain has been mental as well as physical.

It is obviously easier if there is somebody else at the other end matching wicket for wicket, keeping the pressure on the batsmen. Spinners will say the same thing. They like to bowl in harness in the way that David Allen and John Mortimore complemented each other for Gloucestershire or Tony Lock and Jim Laker for Surrey, or Ray Illingworth and Don Wilson for Yorkshire. Would Laker, for all his great off-spinning ability and command of his craft have been quite so successful without Lock? Or *vice versa*? It is interesting to speculate and personally I think each would have lost some effectiveness.

In the same way batting becomes easier if two batsmen are going well at the same time, both attacking the bowling, matching run for run, neither giving the bowlers the slighest respite or hope. A problem halved is far more simple to overcome.

There is another side to a "pairing." Nobody wants to look a dunce. From a team point of view it does not matter who takes the wickets so long as they are falling. Everyone is pleased whoever is picking up the victims. But if one fast bowler happens to get among the wickets this naturally acts as a spur to the other. It makes him strive that little bit harder which benefits the side as a whole.

I have emphasised this point to explain why I got so much pleasure from my first MCC tour to the West Indies at the start of 1968. There was a cricketing bonus to add to the delight of tasting a new way of life and spending three months in the Caribbean. For that was one tour on which I did have a regular partner. In fact it was even better than that. There was a three-way partnership between David Brown, Jeff Jones and myself which made life so much easier and rewarding, and made the future look much more secure from an England point of view.

We were all born within a few months of each other and after the way we worked together during those three months I could see no reason why we should not continue to be a threat to other sides for three or four years to come. Tragically the triangle was broken up within a few months of our return. A left elbow injury cut short the career of Jeff, and the pressure of giving everything he had day in day out gradually reduced the effectiveness of Dave.

But that was later. At the time we had no such worries. We were doing what we wanted to do, bowling in harness, often on wickets offering us encouragement, pace and bounce which enabled us to match our ability against some of the finest stroke-makers in the world. We surprised the folks back home who had bid us farewell on Boxing Day – the season of goodwill – without giving us a chance.

Rohan Kanhai hadn't given us much of a chance either. At least he tried to put in some propaganda work so far as I was concerned when I met him towards the end of the 1967 summer in England at a party given by Bill Tucker, a surgeon who specialises in cricket injuries and has put more than one cricketer back in business when he has been worn out and run down under the demands of the game.

Rohan's opening broadside over a couple of whiskies was far from friendly. "We'll smash you all over the park when we get you on those wickets in the Caribbean," he told me. Not once but several times. It rather took me aback for there was no doubt that he meant it. I could only say something on the lines of "We'll see."

His remarks were similar to others we received when we arrived in Barbados, where a steel band throbbed out a welcome, although there were friendly wishes too.

I was immediately struck by the intense interest and curiosity of the West Indians. Wherever we went they demanded to know who each of us was, what we did, how we did it and so on. Waiters, porters, taxi drivers, airport officials, people in the street, spectators at the net sessions were all the same. And all equally convinced that "we'll thrash you, man," which was usually their opening and parting gambit.

At the start of the tour the West Indies called upon very much the same side that had well beaten us 3–1 in England 18 months earlier. Conrad Hunte had gone but Sobers, Nurse, Butcher and Kanhai remained of the batsmen, aided by newcomer Clive Lloyd. Gibbs and Holford still provided the spin, Hall and Griffith the pace, the last two showing, however, as the tour went on, that they were on the slippery slope down the other side of the hill.

We won the series 1–0, a victory we achieved mainly as a result of a declaration by Sobers but a victory magnificently earned for all that, in particular by Colin Cowdrey once he had been convinced – mainly by Ken Barrington – that such an end was possible. His innings of 71 on the final afternoon of the fourth Test was one of the finest to come from even his prolific and talented bat. It was a narrow series win in the end but we were undoubtedly the better side and might have won the rubber 3–1.

Once Dave, Jeff and myself had teamed up, Colin was able to use us as fast bowlers should be used – firing in short bursts. At the start he would "perm" any two from three with the new ball, each bowler taking a turn at bowling with the wind at his back. When the going became harder, the ball older and softer, he would use us in three or four-over bursts from one end as the strike force with Derek Underwood, Fred Titmus, Basil D'Oliveira, Pat Pocock and Tony Lock doing a stock bowling, containing job at the other. All the while he was able to keep the pressure on the batsmen, even on the placid Bridgetown wicket in Barbados where Geoff Boycott made a double century in the island match, and then complained bitterly when he was out that he had missed valuable batting practice. In every way it was a most satisfying tour, especially for me as the wide-eyed innocent on my first official trip abroad. I stood at the back, watching and noting, taking it all in for future reference. Not only how a touring party conducts itself abroad, but the broader spectrum of life in the West Indies with its contrasting mixture of opulence and poverty.

The tour did not start too well for me. I was never going to get a place in the side for the first Test on the magnificent Port of Spain ground in Trinidad. This is one of the prettiest grounds in the world, set against the tree-covered mountain slopes over which the rain clouds roll, enabling the local weather experts to time the interruptions almost to the minute. These interruptions are usually violent and swift, but the heat is such that it is often possible to play again within minutes of the clouds blowing away.

In the pre-Test run-in, Dave and Jeff had been earmarked for the two fast bowlng places in Trinidad and I was not surprised to be left out. The break did me good for by the time the second Test started at Sabina Park in Jamaica I had had a chance to get acclimatised and was in full swing. I could not have had a more sympathetic wicket on which to bowl. It was an amazing strip with a ridge one end and zigzagged by cracks as if it had been struck by a minor earth tremor. A dull, brown desert in an oasis of green on the eve of the match, it shone like a mirror on the first morning of the game. Amazingly the edges of the cracks stayed firm when we batted first, despite the pounding they took. But the wicket looked like crazy paving before the cement is added by the time the West Indies batted and a large crack had appeared along the top of the ridge. It was a near-lethal strip and it was no surprise to find the West Indies following on.

I have always possessed the knack of being able to get the ball to rise sharply from just short of a length – not an advantage when bowling in front of some umpires who cannot seem to distinguish between a cricket ball bouncer and the dance hall variety – and in Jamaica the ability was magnified whenever a good length ball caught the facing edge of the ridge. It would rear up like a rocket.

It was a day to be on the back foot so far as personal safety was concerned, but not if the batsman wanted to build an innings. If the ball caught the other edge of the ridge – facing the batsman – then it would shoot along the ground just inches high. It was impossible for the batsman to judge what was going to happen. Just a fraction of an inch difference in length between two deliveries brought completely different reactions. In the circumstances it was hardly surprising that I picked up seven for 49, which put me well on the way towards establishing a record return of 27 wickets for an England bowler on a tour of the Caribbean.

For the opportunity to achieve that feat I must thank Dave and Jeff, who each finished with 14 Test wickets on the tour. Statistically they may not have been as successful as I was, but they both contributed greatly towards my total by taking much of the pressure off me and keeping the pressure on the batsmen.

Jeff was particularly nasty on that Jamaica pitch. His left-arm over-the-wicket style posed problems anyway by slanting the ball across the right-handed batsman towards the slips. The wicket conditions made him even more dangerous as the batsmen tried to get behind the ball. It was even worse for Clive Lloyd, a left-hander, and his height proved a great disadvantage.

Jeff's angle of delivery meant that he was bowling the ball into Clive's body. With the ball rearing sharply off a good length it often resulted in Clive trying to fend it away from the underside of his chin. Time and again he threw his bat down in disgust when rapped painfully on the knuckles, hands, arms and body, and stood glaring down the wicket at Jeff.

Dave, too, was hard for the batsmen to counter. I believe he was at his peak on that tour. He is an uncomplicated bowler, relying on his strength to work up his pace and his stamina to keep him going for a long period. He had both in abundance in that series.

Strangely we came close to losing that second Test despite our efforts over the first three days in making the West Indies follow on 233 runs behind. The reason had nothing to do with cricket, strictly speaking.

The direct cause of the switch of fortunes was a riot by an angry crowd, another new experience for me but one I was to meet on every subsequent MCC tour. It destroyed the mood we had built up, and gave the West Indies a chance to take a breather and reassess the situation at a crucial time. I give them credit for taking their escape route well.

Looking back on it, the attempts by the police to quell the unruly mob on the popular side became a farce more in keeping with a theatrical show. But it was far from funny at the time.

The riot was sparked off by Basil Butcher's dismissal in the second innings, the fifth man out with the West Indies still some 30 runs short of making us bat again. He attempted a leg glance against Basil D'Oliveira, got a thin edge and Jim Parks threw himself to his left to take a leg-side catch. There was no question of Butcher not being out and, indeed, he started to walk before the umpire gave the decision.

The edge was so thin that nobody more than a few yards away could hear the ball touch the bat and the catch was not easy to see by those on the popular side watching from a deep mid-wicket position. But there was Butcher on his way with only the tail-enders left to keep Sobers company in his effort to save the match.

First one can was tossed over the 10-feet high wire netting around the boundary edge on that side of the ground. Then a bottle. More cans, more bottles, sticks and stones swiftly followed. Colin Cowdrey tried to pacify the crowd but merely became an extra target. It was time for us to retreat, disappearing into the pavilion while the khaki-clad police, riot squad and, eventually, the tear gas experts took the field.

Instead of quietening the rioters, they just presented extra targets and the order came to fire off the tear gas. That was THE great mistake. The man in charge of the police, a comical stocky little figure in shorts, with a bamboo cane tucked under his left arm and strutting the field like a pocket general, forgot to take into account the direction of the wind. The tear gas canisters sailed over the fence into the popular side – and the rioters stood laughing as the gas was blown away from them back over the ground.

In the press box, next to the popular side, the cricket writers were coughing and spluttering their reports back as the first wave of tear gas hit them before sweeping over the rest of the ground. Soon the mad scramble was on. The authorities ordered the evacuation of the "posh" stands and pavilion but nobody needed telling as men, women and children raced for the inadequate exits. Many women and children were injured as they joined the mobs scrambling over the surrounding brick walls which were all topped with strands of barbed wire. It was everyone for himself.

We were still in the dressing room, with doors and windows closed in an attempt to keep out the tear gas but it still seeped through.

We covered our faces with wet towels, shirts, shorts – anything. I stood under one of the showers as chaos reigned.

The whole thing turned out to be a disaster for us. The mood changed, and it was not possible for Colin or anybody else in the party to recreate the tension and victory spirit when the game eventually resumed the following day in a near empty stadium. This was a sixth day arranged to make up for the time lost as a result of the riots. In fact we very nearly lost the match. Only a delay caused when Jim Parks was struck in the throat and felled by a ball from Wes Hall robbed the West Indies of the time needed to bowl us out after a brilliant match-saving century from Gary Sobers.

While we were facing these last few overs we should have been flying from Jamaica on our way to Antigua. There was only one flight a day from Kingston and this was held up for nearly three hours – everything stops for cricket in the Caribbean – to allow us to complete our escape. We were thankful but the American and Canadian holiday-makers who formed the bulk of the passenger list were not very happy when we eventually climbed on board. Even when we explained the situation to them they could not understand how a game had caused such a fuss.

Looking back on the tour I do not know which was worse, sampling that riot or living through the last few tense and dramatic overs later on in the final Test in Georgetown when the West Indies were pressing for victory to square the series on the sixth day.

Our dressing room was an amazing sight during those final minutes especially when Jeff Jones went out to face the last over of the game from Lance Gibbs, who was getting through his overs so quickly he was almost perpetual motion. No doubt he was acting on the theory that the more balls he sent down, the greater the chance of one of them getting through or finding the edge, especially against tail-enders. A little less haste and more guile could have proved more rewarding from Lance's point of view.

Jeff was our last man and I don't think anybody could bear to watch. It was not that we lacked faith in Jeff, but his previous six innings in the series had brought him only six runs and, at one stage of his career, he had taken more wickets than he had scored runs. That takes some doing after five or six seasons in the game.

Jeff, however, had some "Dutch courage" on board and greeted Alan Knott with a chorus of "We'll keep a welcome in the hillside" on the way out to the middle. I didn't look during that last over. Almost everybody else was hiding in corners, in the toilets or on the floor and even physiotherapist Jack Jennings hid under his massage table.

As in Jamaica we all had towels over our heads, only this time to muffle the deafening sound of the crowd appealing hopefully with every ball bowled. All we knew about what was happening came from "Ollie" Milburn who relayed what he saw as he stuck his head over the window ledge after each huge shout. Then, suddenly, it was all over. Jeff had survived, the match was drawn, the tour was won, the whole three months worthwhile.

Yet the tour ended on a sour note. We had to undergo a hail of stones and abuse from some bitterly disappointed West Indies supporters as we packed our bags and prepared to leave a cricket ground for the last time on the tour. Fortunately, police on horses who had produced a type of rodeo show during the match by patrolling the compact Georgetown Oval from inside the boundary fence, were on hand to clear a path to our cars. It was like a cavalry charge through enemy positions. Even then some youngsters tried to pull our bags out through the open rear windows of our estate wagons as we drove away. Tony Lock, one of the last to leave the pavilion, was hit on the head by a stone and none of us breathed easily until we were well down the road in a cloud of dust.

I suppose it was appropriate that our two worst moments on the tour should take place in Jamaica and Guyana. In both places there was an underlying feeling of tension and we always sensed that it needed just a little spark for violence to erupt.

In Jamaica there were such extremes in the pattern of life and there did not seem to be any middle ground between them. There were the shanty-towns of down-town Kingston, wooden huts crowded one on top of another without sanitation or running water. These gave way to the plush tourist hotels on the edge of the town and the paradise homes halfway up the Blue Mountain range which forms a backcloth to the capital.

Only the brave, the foolhardy and the innocent among the tourists risked walking around at night, when being in pairs was no guarantee of safety. Our time in Kingston was spent mainly in the belt of hotels for tourists. I understand from the lads who went there with Mike Denness on the next tour that the situation had deteriorated. Most free nights we spent sitting in the team hotel, or popping a few hundred yards for a drink in the next hotel, just to change the scenery.

We found these extremes of life everywhere we went on the island, from Kingston to the rich tourist spots of Ocho Rios and Montego Bay, which attract Americans by the plane-load and where even the medium-priced hotels charged £20 to £30 a night – without breakfast – even in 1968.

In Montego Bay, across the other side of the island from Kingston, we sampled the luxury life ourselves when we spent a day at the home of the late William Hill, who took three months away from his bookmaking empire every year to visit the Caribbean. It was a lazy day spent in the company of Lester Piggott, as we relaxed by the swimming pool perched on the hillside, with enough food and drink to have our fill for a week.

That was one side of life. We saw the other on the journey to and from Mr Hill's house, as our cars passed through clusters of wooden huts half way up the hill, the occupants living off the scraps of the rich people. The homes were simple in construction, normally just four walls with an additional room added whenever a new arrival was born. It was easy to understand the resentment of many of the Jamaicans when they were forced to scratch an existence out of nothing while watching the rich at play. Easy to understand their feelings when they saw so much money being poured into the simple task of developing the tourist trade while development of other resources was held back by a shortage of cash.

If the Caribbean provides the setting for one of the prettiest grounds in the world in Queen's Park Oval, Trinidad, it also houses one of the worst in Sabina Park, Kingston. A cramped ground, it is so narrow that Wes Hall has been known to start his run by pushing himself off from the concrete wall at one end which doubles as a sightscreen and a press box.

The pavilion apart, there are no facilities, so that the main pathway around the ground is littered by tradesmen building open fires on which to cook their "pies and pasties" to sell to the crowd. On a steamy day with the stands packed, the atmosphere inside the ground can be frightening, a cauldron which invites trouble when neighbour disagrees with neighbour over a cricketing issue.

Along one side of the ground is a small double-decker stand of cheaper seats where spectator climbs upon spectator until there is no room to move. The stand itself forms the boundary edge and fielding in front of it should command danger money. Although wire netting prevents the spectators in the lower stand from getting on to the playing area there is nothing to stop those in the upper deck reaching over to drop rubbish on the head of an unlucky fielder below. Nót only rubbish but spittle too, and poor Geoff Boycott's head, with a bald patch then beginning to appear at the back, was often a target.

In Georgetown racial tension was caused by the two basic groups themselves battling for power. There were those of Asian background who formed the majority of the population and those of Negro background who held office. Again the poverty was everywhere to be seen, only this time there was not such a sharp contrast of wealth as Georgetown is not a tourist area. This meant, however, that the standard of hotel was poor and it was not unknown for us to wait three or four hours for our evening meal and then still end up with a snack taken in frustration.

The tension could be felt wherever we went and it does not surprise those of us who have toured there to learn that Georgetown is now a centre of political unrest in the Caribbean, and that it is taking a stand against sportsmen who have appeared in South Africa.

A walk at night was a mission of danger and most of our time was spent inside the hotel which was situated on the edge of the main town. Much of Georgetown on our side of the town was pretty, the early colonial influence plainly in evidence in the houses, mainly wooden in construction.

Even a walk in daylight hours carried a certain risk, the walker easy prey for the "choke and rob" gangs. Their method of operation was for one member of the gang to steal up behind the victim and choke him – or her – while his accomplices rifled through pockets and purses.

Generally the standard of hotels we used in the Caribbean was more than satisfactory, but we also experienced for ourselves the tremendous double standards that exist when we played a three-day match in Antigua. The hotel was a disaster.

After the first day's play we had to rush back and change ready to attend a reception. There were no facilities at the ground for having a decent shower so it meant a quick dash to the hotel only to discover that there was no hot water in sink or showers and the cold tap produced nothing else but sea water, heavily salted at that. There was nothing else we could do but strip off and jump in the hotel swimming pool to cleanse ourselves of the sweat and dust. I was a little more unfortunate than the rest. I had been given the match off and spent the second half of the day on the beach. I had omitted to shave in the morning and there was no way that I was going to shave in the evening in salt water. I was forced to go to the reception complete with my day's growth.

The visit to Antigua was marked by an amusing but sad incident involving "Ollie" Milburn as he went out to bat with Geoff Boycott on a wicket lovingly prepared over two years by prisoners from the nearby jail, whose spell inside also found them doing duty as groundsmen on the wicket on the island.

Geoff took first strike leaving "Ollie" at the non-strikers' end where he was given a grand welcome by the umpire. "We're very glad to see you here Mr Milburn," he told "Ollie." "We've heard all about you and been looking forward to seeing you bat. It is indeed an honour for the people of Antigua to have the opportunity to see a batsman of your reputation." "Ollie" was very flattered. His feelings soon changed.

He found himself facing when Geoff took a single in the first over. He played confidently forward to the first ball, got a thick inside edge on to his pad and was surprised to hear a leg before appeal. Even more staggered when he looked up and saw his umpire "friend" shoot his right arm upward like a rocket. So much for the honour of seeing "Ollie" bat.

The whole tour presented a fascinating insight into the lives of other people, an education as well as a pleasure for me, the wide-eyed newcomer. Sampling the luxury, enjoying the beaches of Barbados, the beauty of St. Lucia, the carnival-charged atmosphere of Trinidad with its steel bands and calypso singers, I also saw the poverty that went with it, a poverty which embraced the majority of the people so that a cricket tour provided a rare moment of excitement in their lives.

I was the innocent, too, in the cricketing sense. Standing back and letting the others make the decisions, I accepted their findings as the results of their experience. I stood back, a mere observer, in Trinidad at the tea interval on the final day of the match we won, as the players disagreed among themselves as to whether Sobers' declaration had given us a chance of winning. Colin Cowdrey was unsure, and others were of a like mind. Ken Barrington was frantically convinced this was too good an opportunity to miss, especially with Charlie Griffith unable to bowl, and we should grab it, swinging others round to his point of view by the strength of his argument, until Colin himself became convinced. From such a doubtful scene victory was born, the whole three-month exercise became a success.

1968: Frustrations and disappointments

IT'S HARD to imagine a summer with the Australians visiting England as an anti-climax but that is exactly how I found 1968 on my return from the Caribbean. A summer of frustration, with the weather allowing the Australians to escape with a draw in a series England largely dominated, the fortunes of Sussex declining still further despite an appearance in the Gillette Cup final and the five months disappointment capped by the cancellation of the MCC tour to South Africa.

Throughout the long trek homeward from Georgetown, Guyana, to England early in April, we had been celebrating and talking through the victory in the West Indies, looking forward eagerly to taking on the Australians two months later in the first Test at Old Trafford. When we regrouped in Manchester, however, the spark was missing.

Colin Cowdrey had been impressed with the team spirit he had found in the Caribbean when the party had united and grown in strength from being a single unit. It was an atmosphere he had attempted to recreate when fourteen of us reported to Old Trafford. Unhappily having fourteen caused only confusion on the first morning when the time came to select the actual eleven. There were so many variations from which to choose and in the event England finally selected the wrong one.

The result was a 159-run defeat on a wicket helping the slower bowlers with Bob Cowper, bowling his rarely used off spinners, Johnny Gleeson and Alan Connolly being the main destroyers. Pat Pocock did his best to rescue us with six wickets in the Australian second innings but he lacked support. He could have done with the help of Tom Cartwright or Derek Underwood who had both been left behind in the dressing room. That was the start of our frustrations and typical of how the summer was to continue for me.

The whole feeling was summed up when I found myself in the showers at Old Trafford alongside Alan Knott towards the end of the first Test match. Knotty commented: "It's hard to imagine this being a Test match." I knew exactly how he felt. The sun was missing, so was the crowd. The lack of both meant there was no atmosphere at all over the five days. Manchester in June was a far cry from Georgetown in April.

For me the summer of 1968 on a Test level is best remembered by three innings, the final one being that of Basil D'Oliveira when he was suddenly recalled to the Test side at the Oval in August and helped us to draw the series with 158, an innings which was to have such a dramatic effect on the world of cricket.

Before that had come Colin Milburn's knock in the first innings at Lord's in the second Test match on a flier of a wicket when he stood up manfully to a painful battering from Graham McKenzie in scoring 83 runs. The wicket was green, the ball was coming through between rib and head high but "Ollie" took the lot, rather as Brian Close had done against Wes Hall in the match against the West Indies on the same ground in 1963. "Ollie" hooked successfully whenever he had the opportunity and that innings plus the century he was to score some nine months later in Karachi demonstrated what a loss he was to be to English cricket when he was robbed of an eye by a car accident early in the 1969 summer.

But for the rain England would have won that Test match for we bowled Australia out for 78 and had them following on some 273 runs behind. We would have won the next game at Edgbaston too, but for the loss of the entire first day and most of the third due to the weather. In between the rains came another fine innings, this time from Colin Cowdrey, celebrating his 100th Test appearance with a century. It was a memorable performance for Colin had played the last two thirds of his innings virtually on one leg, a pulled muscle leaving him limping and unable to run.

His injury had still not cleared by the time the fourth Test was played at Headingley, a match remarkable in that the game was more or less conducted by two people who were not taking part. On the Wednesday before the match Colin thought there was a chance of playing but finally had to pull out after failing a fitness test on the Thursday morning with Tom Graveney taking over. Bill Lawry, Australia's captain, had injured a hand at Edgbaston and he too decided against playing on the last morning, leaving Barry Jarman in charge.

After being outplayed in the previous two Tests, Australia held their own at Headingley with Graveney and Jarman doing the sparring out in the middle, Cowdrey and Lawry providing the technical advice from the dressing rooms. It meant that we still had a series to save when we reported one down to the Oval for the final Test. Even there the weather did its best to cheat us.

It was the Test of the rainstorm at lunchtime on the final day which left the Oval resembling a lake just when we needed another five wickets. Time was on our side with only John Inverarity left of the main batsmen and victory looked a pure formality.

I must confess we had given up hope by the time the rain had stopped and there was hardly a blade of grass to be seen. Most of us had started to pack our bags believing the series had got away. Except Colin Cowdrey, that is. Like a modern-day King Canute he rolled up his trousers, waded into the water which was an inch deep in places, and supervised the mopping up operations of hundreds of volunteers. The first drop of rain had fallen just before lunch and the cause still seemed lost when we eventually took the field just before half past five to start Deadly Derek Underwood's finest hour.

Nothing happened for almost 40 minutes as Colin tried every combination he could think of on a dead and saturated wicket. He started with me and rang the changes until Basil D'Oliveira made the first breakthrough when bowling Barry Jarman. Even then victory seemed impossible with only 36 minutes left and another four wickets wanted.

The pictures of those final scenes rank alongside those taken of the leg-trap field on Douglas Jardine's "bodyline" tour of Australia as some of the most remarkable in the history of the game. Derek was a lonely figure at one end with the batsman barely distinguishable at the other among the circle of nine fielders plus wicketkeeper Alan Knott. We were all so close we could have joined hands and played "ring-a-roses" as Derek chipped away, eventually taking the last wicket – that of opening batsman Inverarity – with only six minutes left. It was a remarkable victory to enable us to draw the series. A rare moment of triumph that summer.

If my days with England had been frustrating they were still a joy compared to the happenings at Sussex whenever I returned between Test duties. Each time I was to find the county side at a lower ebb, with the team on a down slide of the switchback we rode in the 1960s.

I mentioned earlier that when I first came into the county side we had a chance of winning the championship in 1963 and might well have done so had we possessed a top quality spinner during the second half of the summer. A spinner would have given us a better chance of bowling out the opposition twice and winning our last three home matches that season. Instead we were held to a draw each time and had to settle for fourth place behind a Yorkshire side taking the title again in the first year of Brian Close's captaincy.

The following year we had slipped to ninth in the championship and by the end of 1965 we were down to 16th. In the year of "Tiger" Pataudi we had risen to 10th, but we dropped three places when Jim Parks took over the captaincy in 1967 and spent most of 1968 down around the bottom of the table.

Frankly the side just was not good enough. Neither, in my opinion, was the leadership on the field. But it didn't start and end there. I feel that the real fault lay with the Sussex committee for their lack of guidance, initiative, communication, drive and general handling, which affected the growth of the club and team spirit. The confusion bred frustration in the dressing room.

Most of the players taken on the staff at the time were not up to standard. Apart from Peter Graves and the newly arrived Tony Greig, there were no batsmen to take the place of Ted Dexter, Ken Suttle and Alan Oakman, who had either retired or were growing towards the end of their careers. And no support was forthcoming for Tony Buss, Don Bates and myself following the retirement of Ian Thomson at the end of a wonderful career.

Sussex had even allowed Barry Richards to slip through their fingers when the door was opened during the winter of 1967–68 for overseas players to step into the game on an immediate registration. He wanted to come to us when Gloucestershire – for whom he had played a season of second eleven cricket – signed up Mike Procter instead.

Yet Sussex dillied, dallied and finally turned down the chance to match the Hampshire bid. Sussex offered Richards £700 and put the offer in writing. Hampshire telephoned an offer of £900 plus the air fare. What a difference Richards would have made to our side if he had come to us in the summer of 1968.

We have since missed out on Rhodesian Paddy Clift who has made such a great impact with Leicestershire. Originally Paddy wrote to Sussex for a chance and assumed we were not interested when he did not receive an immediate reply. We were interested all right. It was just that the secretary put Paddy's letter in his pocket and went off on holiday. It was too late to obtain Clift by the time his holiday was over.

The feeling of hopelessness among the senior players had started before Jim Parks took over the captaincy in 1967 and his appointment did little to stem it. There was not a good feeling in the dressing room and more than one story appeared in newspapers hinting of a player revolt during the early stages of 1968. Inevitably my name was linked with some of the stories but I for once was far away when Jim suddenly announced he was giving up the captaincy half way through that summer. Far away engaged in a Test match, but I wasn't surprised when I heard the news.

I wasn't surprised either when Sussex announced that Mike Griffith was taking over the captaincy. Nor were the rest of the players.

We realised he would be the next choice and Sussex had been

grooming him for the role. He was part of the Sussex syndrome. The son of Billy Griffith, secretary of MCC, former Sussex player and captain, a man with a distinguished war record. Mike himself had won a cricket blue at Cambridge in 1963, 1964 and 1965 as well as blues for hockey and racquets, which indicated he was a very good ball player.

We accepted his appointment although I personally felt that carpenter's son Tony Buss, who was some four years older, vastly more experienced and an excellent reader of the game, would have been a better choice at the time.

I had nothing against Mike. I'd spent many a pleasant evening with him before his appointment but would have preferred Tony purely on cricketing grounds.

In talking to him I never felt Mike had the type of cricketing brain a captain requires. He showed very little tactical flair and lacked vision. He did not understand the way people played, the fields required, or which bowlers were best for certain situations, and could not assess the way a game was shaping. The events in the Gillette Cup final that summer seemed to prove me right.

With a bye in the first round we needed only three matches to get to the final and those games made a refreshing change from our miserable time in the championship in which we slumped to the bottom of the table. Victories over Derbyshire, Northants and Gloucestershire took us back to Lord's and into the final for the first time since winning the trophy two years in succession. Warwickshire provided the opposition.

We should have won the trophy for the third time, especially after an innings of 57 from Jim Parks, supported by Tony Greig making 41, had carried us to 214 for seven by the time our overs ran out. It looked good enough for victory when Warwickshire slumped to 155 for six in reply and needed another 60 from their remaining 13 overs, a rate of nearly five an over.

That was when Alan Smith came in to join Dennis Amiss. He started to hit out boldly, slicing the ball repeatedly over and through the covers, and took Warwickshire home by four wickets. We helped him considerably by not setting the right field or using the right bowlers in an effort to contain him. It was a clear indication of Mike lacking an understanding of the way batsmen played and an ability to assess the way the game was shaping.

The trophy slipped out of our grasp and Cyril Washbrook had no difficulty in naming Alan Smith the man of the match, an award that nearly went to Michael Buss who had scored 36 runs in our innings and followed up by dismissing John Jameson, Rohan Kanhai, Billy Ibadulla and Neal Abberley with his left-arm medium paced bowling. If the result had gone the other way, Michael Buss would undoubtedly have been the hero of Lord's that afternoon instead of slipping away with the rest of us to drown our sorrows.

Apart from securing my place in the England side when playing in all five Test matches after my winter of joy in the West Indies, the summer of 1968 holds no particular pleasant memories for me.

Worse was to follow later in September with the refusal of the South African Government to accept Basil D'Oliveira as a member of the MCC party, after he had been added to the list following the withdrawal of Tom Cartwright with a shoulder injury.

Missing South Africa was a great disappointment. Not only from a touring viewpoint but because it ended any showdown with the South African side who were claiming at the time to be the best in the world.

The victory in the Oval Test match against Australia had brought the memories of the Caribbean flooding back and we felt we were capable of upsetting South Africa's boast despite the presence of the Pollock brothers, Eddie Barlow, Mike Procter, Barry Richards and Dennis Lindsay in their side, to say nothing of Colin Bland.

It was a measure of Basil's popularity with the team that nobody ever blamed him or questioned his right to be in the tour party despite, for him, a lean summer in 1968, when he was dropped after the first Test and reappeared for the final game only when illness caused a change in the original selection.

There was, of course, no question of England backing down and being dictated to by the South African Government as to the make-up of the side. Basil had just as much right to be in the team as any other member despite the fact that he had been born in Cape Town of Cape coloured parents. If they would not accept him, there was no alternative than to call off that particular tour, but I question the wisdom of breaking off all official cricketing ties with South Africa and throwing their game into isolation.

I am against apartheid and all it stands for, but does it change the situation by turning your back on it and on the people in cricket over there who are equally opposed to separatism? I doubt it.

Has it yet changed? On the surface possibly, as demonstrated by the token gesture in allowing West Indian John Shepherd of Kent and Pakistan-born Younis Ahmed of Surrey to tour with the Derrick Robins side in the autumn of 1974. They received a great welcome whenever they stepped onto a first-class field with us, black and white together, the crowd rising to salute their presence. Many people told me they never expected to see black and white mixed in a first-class match.

But has it changed deep down? Have the lives of the black Africans been improved? The answer must be: "No." It will take more than isolating South African cricket to solve the complexities of the country's system.

1968–69: Pakistan riots – "Thanks, Basil"

So no South Africa that winter of 1968–69. Just Ceylon and Pakistan instead. A year after witnessing the extremes between luxury and poverty in the Caribbean I was to see it again at close hand in Pakistan where the contrast is even more marked, with only a small percentage of the population enjoying a standard of living we would find acceptable in Britain. The three months in the West Indies had increased my thirst for travelling and studying different life-styles as well as having increased my cricketing experiences.

Unhappily I was to lose one of my West Indies companions during my second tour. The final Test in Georgetown had signalled the end of my partnership with Jeff Jones. During the last game in Guyana he had complained of a sore elbow when throwing in a ball from the boundary. Back in England, before he had time to bid for a place against Australia, his left elbow started playing up and he was ordered to rest.

By the end of the summer he was back bowling fast again and looked to have made a complete recovery. That was good enough for the England selectors who, recalling his West Indian deeds, lost no time in teaming Jeff up with David Brown and myself for the substitute tour of Ceylon and Pakistan. It was not to last.

It was in Ceylon that Jeff's cricket career finally came to an end when his elbow gave way again under the strain and he was sent home – tears in his eyes – flying out of the first-class game for good. I felt deeply sorry for him . . . there but for the grace of God. My troubles later were minor by comparison though they seemed big at the time. In Lahore I was dropped from the Test side for the first time as a disciplinary measure, although only a very few people are aware of it even today.

Before we had arrived in Pakistan the tour was in a shambles, the MCC party being used as a political pawn again – so soon after the South Africa affair – with our manager Les Ames caught right in the middle. He was in a terrible position, being pressed by the Pakistan authorities to continue with the tour because they saw it as a means of keeping the peace, and being urged by the

British High Commission staff to stay while most of us felt it would be wiser to go home.

Throughout our fortnight in Ceylon we had read reports of how riots were spreading throughout the East and West wings of Pakistan and when we arrived in Karachi we found the city under a dusk-to-dawn curfew. Part of the East Pakistan schedule had been cancelled because of rioting, killing and looting and matches had been re-arranged in territories we knew nothing about. Instead of going into the centre of the city we booked into a hotel only a mile or so from the airport, ready to make a quick dash to safety if any more trouble arose.

After several conferences with the Pakistan authorities, Les Ames settled on a new itinerary which would take us out of the main trouble spots for ten days in order to give the situation time to settle down and the police and army a chance to re-establish law and order. It is no coincidence that the places we visited were Ayub Khan strongholds and we were doing his "thank you" duty.

Where politics and sport became mixed to a scandalous degree was in our visit to Dacca in East Pakistan, now known as Bangladesh. When there had been a doubt about our arrival, Dacca had been removed from the schedule because it was considered too dangerous. Once we were in Pakistan however, it was quickly put back on the itinerary as the setting for the second of the three Test matches. This followed anti-government demonstrations when the idea was first raised of a possible breakaway movement and the setting up of an independent country.

Not only did the Pakistan Government use us, but sometimes it seemed the British authorities did so too. Most of us had been in Georgetown a year before and sampled the tension of a country torn by internal rumblings. Pakistan was far, far worse. We were all distinctly unhappy about the visit to East Pakistan but were assured by the British High Commission staff in Dacca that all would be well. Right up to the last moment Les Ames checked on the situation and each time he was told we would be safe, that order had been restored to the capital.

Imagine our surprise, anger and dismay when we finally arrived in Dacca to find that the police and army authorities had pulled out and were camped on the outskirts leaving the entire place in the hands of the rioting students.

Their greetings were friendly when we arrived. Their warnings were not when we broadcast our disapproval and suggested we would be happier flying straight out the following morning. We were warned in no uncertain terms that our coach would not reach the airport. We had little faith in a senior British High Commission official who attempted to assure us we would come to no harm. He invited us to his home to meet the other British people in East Pakistan over cocktails, still insisting he was right to bring us over. Then he asked us to leave while he had a talk with the rest. It was not until afterwards that we discovered his talk was to discuss evacuation plans in case the situation worsened. And there we were dumped right in the middle of it.

That week in Dacca was probably the most nerve-racking of my life. Day and night we could hear gunfire – some of it only yards from our hotel – as the students patrolled the streets armed with rifles seeking out people they believed to be corrupt. When found, some of these people were bound and gagged and tossed in the river to drown.

At the ground itself the work of stewards was taken over by specially selected students and, happily, the Test itself passed without incident, apart from the occasional fires on the terracing which is part and parcel of cricket matches in Pakistan. But it was impossible to play cricket of any purpose when thinking of one's own safety all the time, waiting for the first sound of rifle fire, the first sign of trouble and wondering where and how it would be possible to escape. We all felt so vulnerable out in the middle where the nearest shelter was provided by the wicket covers.

It was hardly more comfortable off the field. The Dacca Stadium – used for all sorts of sporting activity – was a half-finished concrete shell rising out of a piece of waste ground. The dressing room was hidden under the main stand. Just four bare concrete walls without windows, dark and gloomy, lit by a single 40-watt bulb, with one door leading out to a narrow corridor and the pitch. There was nowhere for us to sit to watch the cricket, nothing to do but stay in and wait, like prisoners in a dungeon awaiting their fate.

The sanitation was primitive, the food inedible, and we existed on oranges and bananas throughout the day, thankful for the tins of relief food we had brought with us from England, until the time came when we had to push our way through the crowds to our coach and the return journey to the hotel. The few yards from the dressing room door to the coach were a nightmare as grubby hands felt over our bodies, searching in pockets for money which could be taken without opposition. There was nothing we could do, as we were forced to walk out carrying our cricket gear high above our heads. We were defenceless, and Colin Cowdrey was robbed of all his loose change. It was a relief when Dacca was behind us and we were flying back to West Pakistan. All the way to the airport we kept looking back over our shoulders wondering if any attempt would be made to stop our flight.

Perhaps the one person we felt sorry for above all others was Colin Milburn who arrived in Dacca right in the middle of these troubles. Colin was not an original member of the tour party but had been sent for as an additional batsman. He had just finished a season playing for Western Australia in the Sheffield Shield competition, was relaxing for a few days on a beach outside Perth and dreaming of his return to England by sea with Graham McKenzie when he received the cable from Lord's asking him to report to Pakistan.

The journey had taken him almost 72 hours with several changes of plane and he caught us up in Dacca at the worst possible time. The day of his arrival happened to coincide with a religious festival during which cows were slaughtered where they stood in the street. We all turned up at the airport to greet Colin, welcoming him with a guard of honour and then driving him away to a hotel. We told him that our hotel, a modern building equipped with air conditioning, swimming pool, luxury bedrooms and two dining rooms was full. We took him to another that had none of these things. After his tiring journey, the street scenes and the stories of the general situation so unnerved Colin that he refused to leave us and came to our net practice instead. Only then did he discover we had been pulling his leg.

So far as home comforts were concerned, the ten days spent up-country at the start of the tour left much to be desired, even though we were away from the main trouble areas. Only once in those ten days did we come across a hotel where we could shower and wash from our bodies the dust and dirt collected from crossing the desert by road in a coach in which the doors and windows did not fit. The rest of the time we spent in Government or factory-owned "Rest Houses" where the people did their best to make us feel welcome, although the size of the party strained their resources and equipment. I don't think any of us ate a square meal during those ten days.

For the first game of that ten-day trek around Multan, Bahawalpur, and Lyallpur we were forced to rise at 5.30 and take a specially chartered plane for a two-hour journey to the ground. Not the best way to prepare for a match. We were behind schedule when we arrived and the match began late when Colin Cowdrey told the local officials that no English side ever started a game of cricket without first having a cup of tea. Two or three times the umpire looked into our dressing room asking when the game would start but Colin insisted on tea first after our journey. He got his way.

There was another cruel dawn start later for our visit to Sahiwal and the last chance of practice before the first Test in Lahore. By that time we had spent a couple of days in our comfortable hotel in Lahore and we were not looking forward to going out into the country again.

Our discomfort was even greater at 5.30 in the morning when we were presented with our coach for the two-hour road journey. One look inside was enough to have manager Les Ames appealing to the English cricket writers accompanying us for the use of a fleet of cars they had hired. The coach had been used as a cattle truck the day before – and given to us complete with all the trimmings of straw and droppings.

In Sahiwal we had been booked into another Government Rest House which had been "condemned" three years previously by Les Ames when he managed the Under-25 tour in Pakistan. He had recommended that MCC should never visit Sahiwal again until the town boasted a decent-sized hotel. I have two great memories of the visit. One is the plate of sixteen eggs David Brown ate before going to a function where we had been warned not to eat the food. These eggs were cooked over an open fire in a smoke filled "kitchen."

The other one was that night – fortunately our only night – in the Rest House, where it was so cold we lit fires in our rooms only to find the chimneys blocked and the smoke choking us.

Despite the hardship, it was an eye-opening experience for me on my first tour to that part of the world. The fascinating but saddening life I saw seemed a million miles away from civilisation as we know it at home. There were many wretched sights of living conditions, people close to starvation, emaciated children. There was plenty to think about in the evenings when we were closeted in rooms we all thought were almost unfit for human habitation, but which would have seemed like palaces to many living not 50 yards away.

The ordeal was still not over when we returned to Lahore for the first Test. We had three days recovery time but for two of these we were confined to our hotel because of demonstrations, many near the hotel which was situated on the main road to the airport being used by officials racing in and out on peace-keeping missions.

We were left with only one day's practice on the eve of the first Test and it was during that net session that Colin Cowdrey came across to me and asked me how I was feeling – a conversation which was to lead to me being left out of the team.

I told him I was perfectly okay but Colin asked me if I would like to bowl off my long run. He wanted to see me bowl flat out after being cooped up for two days. I didn't. I wasn't being awkward or rude. It was just that I thought it completely unnecessary in the hot sun. Also, after two days in which my only activity had been in a pitch and putt competition organised by the players and Press in the hotel grounds, it seemed risky to go flat out straightaway.

It wasn't that I refused point blank. I just carried on with what I was doing and what I thought was best for me, knowing how I felt physically. I wanted to concentrate on finding my rhythm by running about the distance I do in the John Player League. I was still quite sharp at the end of it and confident that I was fully fit to be at my best and fastest in the Test the following day.

My failure to go off my long run was, I learned later, the reason why I was not to play in the first Test. I also understood that Tom Graveney, vice-captain on the tour, was particularly against me playing. I don't know what I had done to upset him apart from not taking him too seriously at times. Tom liked the authority being vice-captain gave him, but was inclined to overdo it on occasions when dealing with the "other ranks."

Over a rare beer in the bar that evening I was given a hint that I might be left out the following day "because of my attitude." Nothing was said to me officially until I went to the ground the next morning. Then Colin came up to me, put his hand on my shoulder and told me I wasn't in the final eleven. No explanation, just a quick word and I found myself sharing twelfth man duties with the other unlucky players.

I must admit I was very disappointed with Colin. Less than twelve months before I had given him everything I had in the West Indies whenever he had asked for it. I'd done the same against the Australians at home in the summer.

It was not as if there had been a doubt about my fitness. I'd played in the three up-country matches which was more than the other opening bowlers Dave Brown and Bob Cottam had done. I'd taken five wickets against Bob's seven while Dave had yet to "strike" on the tour. Yet I was the one to go in the final reckoning.

The saddest feature, I felt, was the fact that Colin did not appear to take my word that I was all right. He seemed to want concrete proof I was fit by asking me to bowl off my long run for half-a-dozen or so deliveries. I am not sure what that would have proved. At the end of it he would still have had to take my word that I was feeling 100 per cent.

I was certainly not messing around in the nets. The odd joke perhaps but nothing more. Maybe David Brown and Bob Cottam had been bowling off their full run but each individual is different. What Dave might have required that day did not necessarily apply to me. I knew exactly what I needed to do to make sure I was in peak condition. Maybe a new captain who didn't know me might have wanted further assurances in some way or other. But I felt that Colin should have been able to trust me, having known me through two complete series during which I had played in nine successive Tests.

On the same theme Brian Statham tells the story of when he was suddenly recalled to test cricket for the final match against South Africa at the Oval in 1965. It is usual in home Test matches for the players to report to the ground around lunch-time on the Wednesday and have a gentle work-out during the afternoon.

The other players had already changed and were out in the field on the far side of the Oval under the Vauxhall Stand when Brian arrived. He didn't bother to change but strolled over to the nets, leant against a post and quietly smoked a cigarette while he watched the others at work.

The selectors were there, including Doug Insole who was the chairman. He asked Brian if he was going to bowl but Brian politely refused the invitation. I gather there were a few odd glances between the selectors but nobody challenged Brian.

He explained later that if he had spent 30 or 40 minutes running around under the hot sun after a 200-mile drive from Manchester he certainly would not have been at his best the next day when England needed him. He was fit and he knew that one practice session wasn't going to make him any better. "Bowling in matches keeps me fit for bowling," he used to say.

Perhaps the Lahore game was a good one to miss for the authorities sectioned off the stand next to the dressing room for Army marksmen equipped with rifles in case of trouble from the cheap seats on the other side of the ground. The one thing they hadn't considered was the players out in the middle if the shooting started. They would have been right in the line of fire!

Fortunately the marksmen had been withdrawn by the time the riot started. Nevertheless we nearly lost the manager when he walked round the boundary to discover the cause of the disturbance and was almost decapitated by half a chair which came hurtling from the terraces and missed the back of his head by no more than six inches.

From the moment we first sampled the atmosphere in Pakistan we had a feeling that one day we would be beating a hasty retreat. That was exactly what happened when the final Test was brought to a quick end in Karachi by demonstrators who swarmed over the ground destroying everything in their path like an army of red ants on the march.

The first two days had been constantly interrupted by cricket demonstrations with the Karachi people protesting at the appointment of Saeed Ahmed as Pakistan captain in place of their favourite Hanif. Much time was lost.

The third day was entirely different. The mood was ugly, the people in Karachi upset by the death of one of the anti-Government leaders, who had been on a fast. As a mark of respect and to signify sympathy with the cause, all cars travelling on the road that day were ordered to fly a black flag. Les Ames refused, rightly, saying that we were a cricket team and could not be used for any political activity. The journey to the ground was tense.

We had been given a truck load of armed troops to escort us from the hotel to the ground but at the first road junction we turned right and the troops went straight on, never to be seen again.

On that third day we were still batting with "Ollie" Milburn and Tom Graveney – leading the side in the absence of Colin Cowdrey who had flown home following the death of his father-in-law – having scored centuries, and Alan Knott nearing his maiden Test hundred, when the demonstrators were spotted marching towards the stadium.

They skirted the main entrance, walked to the other side of the ground and then clambered in, tearing up seats to use as weapons and scattering spectators in their wake. Poor Knotty just could not believe it with his century only four runs away and he had to be dragged from the wicket by David Brown long after the Pakistan players had fled to the safety of their dressing room.

For almost an hour we were locked in our dressing room while the battle raged outside and the decision was taken by the Pakistan Board of Control to abandon the tour. Our escape was made only when the large crowd gathered outside the dressing room were assured that we would be returning as soon as order had been restored.

We were worried they might be become suspicious when we packed all our cricket gear into the waiting cars but they even helped us carry our bags, genuinely upset by the disturbances and the political demonstrators still creating havoc inside the stadium. Our last look at the ground was over our shoulders, smoke still rising from the fires the rioters had started. As the official Pakistan tour brochure said on our arrival: "Thanks Basil D'Oliveira for making this tour possible!"

The demonstration had happened just before the lunch period. By mid-afternoon we were back in our hotel. By midnight we were flying off from Karachi on our way home. Les Ames had managed to get us all booked on the first available flight out and our escape was kept a secret in case an attempt was made to bar our exit. The flight home matched the tour. There was no food or drink on the plane. We were delayed in Cairo because they could not restart the engines. Delayed again in Rome for another couple of hours and finally held up in Paris because London Airport was fogbound. Were we glad to see it when we finally arrived!

By now my cricketing life had come to resemble a ride on the "Big Dipper" scenic railway. The thrill of the climb and the view from the top. The turning of the corners not knowing what was ahead. The plunge to the low spots between times.

The climbs to the top came in the winters. Despite those experiences in Pakistan I enjoyed touring and seeing the world. Tours provided two, three or four months where every move could be planned to achieving the main object – winning the series. In between there were the smaller peaks of Test matches at home, each game a different adventure where what was going to happen next was unsure, even when playing against India, Pakistan and New Zealand, the three weakest countries. Then the lows – for me – of returning to the muddled affairs of Sussex, forever struggling it seemed against the odds. None of us knew where we were going but this was different. It was no adventure because we felt that whatever corner we took with Sussex we knew we would find a blind alley awaiting us. I was more fortunate than the others. I had Test matches as a means of escape, winter tours to satisfy my desires. And there was still Australia ahead.

1969: Dropped again. Illingworth and captaincy

IT WAS not long before I was dropped by England again. That was back home during the summer after the three-match series against the West Indies in the first half of the season.

Officially I was rested for the first match of the following series against New Zealand at Lord's so that the selectors could have a look at Derbyshire's Alan Ward at a Test level. But I soon learned I had been disciplined. Ray Illingworth told me, and I admired him for it.

Ray had taken over as England captain that summer following Colin Cowdrey's unfortunate achilles tendon injury which was to keep him out of the game until the last fortnight of the summer. Under Ray's leadership, England had won the first Test against the West Indies, had finished only 37 runs short of the victory target in the second Test and won the third Test at Headingley to retain the Wisden Trophy we had earned in the Caribbean on my first tour.

With 15 wickets in the series, more than any other bowler, I had expected to stay in the side for the start of the New Zealand Tests. I have no doubt I would have, but for Ray.

He insisted I should be left out for one Test for disobeying his instructions on the last morning of the Headingley game and I was choked when I heard his reason. I felt he was unfair. It was not so much a question of disobeying him as coming to a different conclusion of how best to achieve the same objective – taking the last three West Indies wickets.

Bowled out for 161 in their first innings, the West Indies had made a bid for the 303 needed for victory in their second, thanks mainly to a solid innings of 91 by Basil Butcher. By the last morning they had reduced the target to 73 runs with three tail-end batsmen left. The odds were heavily against them.

There had been speculation overnight about whether Ray would take the new ball in the morning or continue with Derek Underwood, who had bowled well on the fourth evening. Derek had taken four wickets to make the breakthrough, but Ray opted for pace and this is when my troubles started.

"Give me everything you've got for five or six overs," Ray told me at the start. However, after one over I felt the wicket was not responding to sheer speed and I would be more effective if I slowed down a little and attempted to seam the ball. Apart from "Deadly Derek" on the fourth afternoon, the seam bowlers had been the most effective so far – not an uncommon happening at Headingley.

For the West Indies John Shepherd of Kent had been the most dangerous bowler until handicapped by a pulled thigh muscle injury, and we had been thankful he could not bowl in our second innings. For us Barry Knight had been the main wicket-taker in the West Indies first innings with four. These facts influenced me to change from sheer speed to a medium-paced seam style and I did everything but get a wicket with it. It was obviously not to Ray's satisfaction.

What made my decision seem worse from Ray's point of view was that nothing happened for the first half an hour while the batsmen steadily chipped their way over 250. No doubt people were beginning to question his wisdom in taking the new ball. Two wickets sealed my fate in Ray's eyes. Both were snapped up by David Brown steaming in at full pace at the other end, holding nothing back. By then, I had been banished to the boundary and replaced by Derek Underwood, who took the other wicket in England's 30-run victory.

When the side for the first Test against New Zealand was announced I was told by Alec Bedser, chairman of selectors, that I had been rested so that they could have a look at Alan Ward. I wasn't entirely satisfied with that explanation. As a general principle, I think a player should not be dropped just so that the selectors can have a look at an alternative when the opposition is not up to strength. Any player coming into the Test side should be better than the man he replaces, and it is hardly fair on the dropped player to lose his Test match fee when he does not deserve to be left out. There is little enough money around in cricket as it is.

But that was only the reason given to me by Alec Bedser. The real reason came from Ray when he phoned me at my hotel on the Monday evening some 36 hours later. Sussex were playing Essex at Colchester. Ray was playing for Leicestershire at Edgbaston yet he took the trouble to phone me to let me know he had asked for me to be left out because I had not carried out his orders. I did not like what he had to say and told him so, but I was impressed by the fact that he had bothered to get in touch with me to put the record straight.

For the reasons stated earlier, it is not hard to imagine that I was in a furious mood when I put the phone down. I was still far from happy the following morning and somebody had to suffer. It was Essex and Hampshire, but at least Sussex benefited.

On that last afternoon at Colchester I took three quick wickets in my first spell and came back to finish the innings with another three giving me six for 20 off 14 overs in their innings of 141. That was in the middle of July and it brought Sussex their first championship win of the summer. The following match was against Hampshire at Hove. That game was over in two days, Sussex winning again and this time I finished the match with ten wickets – the five in the second innings off a short run – for 80 runs.

Thanks to Ray I was £150 worse off, having lost my Test match appearance money, but Ray was as good as his word. Although England thrashed New Zealand by 230 runs inside four days in that first Test at Lord's I was back in the England side for the second Test, at David Brown's expense. That was the only change but my dropping and my recall established an understanding between Ray and myself.

From that moment I was to know exactly where I stood with him as did every other player who came under his captaincy. He spoke his mind. Just as important, I learned that he was a man of his word.

Incidentally, my dropping cost me more than the Test match fee. During the West Indies game at Lord's some six weeks earlier I had penned in verse my feelings and impressions about what it is like to play at the headquarters of world cricket. A television company heard about my poem and planned to film me bowling during the New Zealand match, using the film as a backcloth with John Betjeman reading my words over the action in a 15-minute clip to be shown on a sports programme that weekend. The fee would have come in handy.

Ray and I still had our differences after that sacking but they were always out in the open. He was never slow to criticise. At the same time he would always listen and take into account my point of view. It was obvious that he considered me a key figure in his victory plans and he allowed me a certain amount of freedom, especially on tour, yet he demanded his pound of flesh in the Test matches. I was willing to give it to him on this basis, and we have understood each other since.

Against the Rest of the World in 1970, for instance, I bowled almost twice as many overs in the series as the next bowler, getting through 38 overs in one innings at Edgbaston and 32 overs in one innings at the Oval. Yet, because of Ray's tactical flair and experience I always felt that I was bowling exactly when I should have been.

Only occasionally did he call upon me to do a stock bowling job with the intention of closing the game up and keeping the runs down. Generally I was used as an out-and-out strike bowler under his command. He harboured and nurtured his bowlers like no other captain I have served. The only other who approached Ray in that respect was Mike Smith back in 1965 when I first came to the Test scene. I thought he was very astute in his handling of players and I would have liked to have played under him more.

In his ability to handle bowlers Ray, of course, had one great advantage over Mike, and over Colin Cowdrey and Mike Denness, too, come to that. Being a bowler himself he was better qualified to understand the problems a bowler faces and react accordingly. From what I read and heard, one of the biggest complaints about the leadership of Mike Denness in the West Indies in 1973–74 concerned the handling of his bowlers, the faster bowlers in particular. They felt that Mike did not understand their needs and wishes, respond immediately to their request for fielding changes or really make any attempt to communicate with them. They seldom had a chance to talk to him about bowling or their requirements.

It must have been difficult for him having had little experience of captaincy in the first-class game at that stage of his life and only a limited knowledge of the demands of the five-day Test match. Taking all that into consideration perhaps it might have been more pertinent to have aimed the criticism at the men who suddenly chose Mike to lead the side in the West Indies when chopping short Ray's Test career. And, from what I understand, it was not only the selectors who were to blame for that decision.

Whatever the rights and wrongs of the situation in the West Indies I had no complaints about Mike's captaincy in his handling of me in the one Test I played under his leadership against the Australians at Edgbaston in 1975. It was to be his last as captain, after putting the Australians in and then losing the match. He was very orthodox in his bowling changes, doing nothing inspired but again nothing in which I could find fault. By then, of course, he had had the experience of two tours and one summer in England behind him.

I am not suggesting that batsmen should not captain sides, but if an all-rounder is available who is worth his place in the team, then so much the better. Tony Greig was the obvious choice to take over from Denness in 1975.

Not that an all-rounder necessarily understands the position fully. Ted Dexter and Brian Close are two captains I have served under who have been classified as all-rounders, although I would really categorise them as batsmen who could bowl a bit. I found them both inclined to be a little dictatorial, introducing too much theory into their leadership. I was never sure with either of them when I would be asked to bowl or when I would be taken off. Sometimes they would bring on a bowler for all the wrong reasons – possibly because they were just plain bored with what was going on. Each must have puzzled keen students of the game at times, but if a change resulted in a wicket it was always hailed as a master stroke, a piece of brilliant inspired leadership.

Gary Sobers struck me as belonging to the same category whenever I watched him handling the West Indies bowling attack or leading Nottinghamshire. I never felt that he had a real feeling for the problems of his bowlers, or any insight in to how they were feeling. He was undoubtedly very fortunate to have Wes Hall and Charlie Griffith plus the off-spin of Lance Gibbs to call upon when the West Indies were regarded as the unofficial world champions. Then again he always had his own outstanding ability to extract himself from difficult situations he may have created by not quite utilising fully the talents of those under him.

There is, of course, a link between Dexter, Close and Sobers which might account for the reason they made similar impressions on me. All three had so much natural ability that playing cricket was so easy for them. It must have been difficult for them to understand the problems ordinary mortals went through when playing cricket. Again all three of them were born gamblers with a passion for horse racing and a liking for the outsider. That, too, might explain their inspired moves and moods on the cricket field, and why they sometimes exasperated the men who played under them.

Once, against Northamptonshire, I painfully recall Ted keeping me going throughout the morning session. He signalled the end of my opening spell by telling me I had one more over. I took a wicket in that over and Ted kept me on. Three or four times in all Ted asked me for "just one more over" and each time I took a wicket. On and on I went until lunch brought a merciful break. Ted should have taken me off when he thought it right to do so in the first place but the capture of a wicket swayed his judgement. From Sussex's point of view I suppose it was a rewarding morning with half the Northants side out in less than two hours but I was of little use to Sussex for the rest of the match or the following game. Ted's maneouvring left me shattered for a week.

Another thing Ted and Closey had in common – and West Indies bowlers told me it applied to Gary as well – was the habit of mysteriously moving fielders in the middle of an over. Sometimes it was only a matter of inches, particularly in Closey's case. Perhaps they spotted something the batsman was doing and were hoping to take advantage of it but unless they communicated their discovery to the bowler, there was little chance of the bowler producing the type of delivery necessary to induce that batsman into making the mistake the skipper was expecting. And they seldom communicated their reasons for changing the field.

Ray's strong point was in quickly guessing the mood and the problems of the bowler. Quite often and for no reason at all a fast bowler may not be able to strike his true rhythm straight away and his bowling suffers. I know this has happened to me on many occasions throughout my career.

To a batsman-captain this may not seem important. To Ray it was an essential issue and he would realise I was struggling almost as soon as I did. There is no point in keeping me on when that happens. Far better to come off even for two or three overs and try again. The second time everything would click and away I would go. Sometimes it happens the other way round. Everything perfect for the first spell, the rhythm missing for the second. Ray would notice and act.

The other advantage arising from him being a bowler was his ability to sum up batsmen: the way they play, technical weaknesses, strong points etc. A particular batsman might be vulnerable to a left-arm over-the-wicket bowler, or on his leg stump, or when driving. Ray might even know where a batsman looked to score his first run to get off the mark. Deny him that type of delivery and the longer he has nought against his name or number, the more anxious he becomes. Ray had a remarkable memory for that sort of detail.

Most of all, because he insisted on his "own" side, he was able to get the best out of his players, both mentally and physically. He built up a tremendous team spirit which stood us in good stead on numerous occasions, nowhere more so than in Sydney during the final Test in Australia on the 1970–71 tour.

As I have said, as a result of his understanding and reading of the game, Ray was able to nurture his bowlers, not only in Australia with Peter Lever, Bob Willis, Ken Shuttleworth and myself but back home when we went into Test matches with only two recognised bowlers.

Falling under Ray's influence in 1969 only helped to highlight the problems when I returned to play for Sussex that summer, the first complete season under Mike Griffith's command and one of improvement in terms of our final place in the county championship.

We jumped ten places from the bottom of the table to finish in seventh position, largely as a result of a grand final flourish when we won our last three home matches, picking up 47 points. That made a total of five victories in all, the two others coming when I was dropped from the England side as described earlier.

The first of those final three victories came against Yorkshire, a match which was to have an unfortunate ending for Geoff Boycott four days before he was due to play in the Gillette Cup final. Fending off a ball from me at Eastbourne he broke a bone in his hand which forced him to miss the final, although his absence wasn't felt on that occasion, Yorkshire beating Derbyshire by 69 runs.

By now bonus points for batting and bowling had been introduced in the championship. Collecting the points for batting was our main problem. Only Gloucestershire, second in the table, collected more bonus points for bowling, but we were well down the list when batting points were totted up. This lack of strength was emphasised in the John Player League when we finished bottom in the first year of the competition.

It was not just Ray's on-the-field performances that impressed me and most of the lads. His record off the field during his five years in charge of the Test side would take some beating. He expected professionalism on the field and wanted it off the field as well. Something I totally agreed with.

He believed he was leading the best side in the world. And he wanted the best treatment and facilities for them in the way of travel, hotels, allowances and dozens of other things. He fought hard to get them and the players appreciated his efforts.

Once he was upset to find himself travelling second class on a train to London when a county club official was travelling first class on the same train. It was during the winter and both were going to London to attend the same cricket committee meeting at Lord's. He reasoned that as they were both doing the same job, travelling to London for the same purpose, and both had equal voting power and rights on that particular committee, it was wrong that there should be this distinction between player and official. I gather he won his point.

On another occasion he was embarrassed when, as England captain, he invited three guests to dinner at the team hotel in London. The guests ordered their dinner first and then it came to Ray's turn. He made his selection from the menu but was told by the waiter – in front of his guests – that he could not have it as the total cost was more than the meal allowance permitted by the MCC.

Naturally on that occasion he paid the extra from his own pocket, but thereafter the members of the England team were allowed to chose from the complete menu instead of being restricted to a limited variety of meals. Ray had insisted this was right. And it was.

Small points perhaps but Ray took up the challenge on behalf of the players on numerous occasions to remove some of the indignities and injustices which players have had to suffer far too long because of the attitude of the powers that be.

I can remember being involved in helping to remove one of those irritations which arose every time we played a Test match at the

Oval. Parking facilities are very limited on the ground and we all appreciated the problem the Oval authorities had in trying to fit everybody in who wanted to take a car.

What we could not understand was why the players were given car parking facilities across the road in the playground of the Archbishop Tennison's School while all sorts of nondescript officials were allowed to take their cars through the Hobbs Gates and almost up to the pavilion steps.

It was not the walk to which we objected, or the crossing of the road, or the pushing through the crowds coming from the Oval tube station and jostling outside the gates. It was just the feeling that we, the players, did not matter.

Needless to say, this sort of constant pressure on our part did not go down well with the authorities (whether at home or overseas) who saw their power being undermined. Gradually Ray and I built up a quota of black marks against our names, a quota later to be held against us.

1970: Rest of the World. More Sussex troubles

AFTER TWO winters overseas, which meant I had been playing cricket almost non-stop since the spring of 1967, I stayed at home for the winter of 1969–70 apart from paying a fleeting visit to the West Indies. There was no MCC tour but plenty of invitations to join private parties which could have kept me travelling all winter. I turned them down.

I felt that I was at the halfway stage of my career and needed the rest to recharge the batteries, especially in view of the tough programme ahead with England due to play five "Tests" against the Rest of the World in 1970 – in place of the cancelled visit by the South African side – followed by the winter in Australia. I think I was wise.

I am very proud of the 19 wickets I took against the Rest of the World, even though, laughably, they have now been officially deducted from my Test playing record. They were earned the hard way against the best batsmen in the world, each trying to upstage the rest. Gary Sobers, Clive Lloyd and Eddie Barlow each scored two centuries in the series and Rohan Kanhai and Graeme Pollock one apiece.

I played in all five games, with a succession of bowling partners. It was tough, very tough, but the whole exercise provided ideal practice for the coming tour of Australia – in marked contrast to the easy passage England enjoyed against India and Parkistan before Mike Denness's team went "down under" in 1974–75. I do not think that easy series helped Mike's campaign in Australia.

We lost against the Rest of the World 4–1, which was not surprising in view of the strength of the opposition. It was heart-breaking bowling against that line-up. Imagine doing well enough to get six or seven batsmen out reasonably cheaply only to find Mike Procter walking to the wicket at number nine, as he did in the first two matches.

Yet the difference between the sides was not as great as the margin would suggest. We might easily have gone into the final game all square for we were convinced we should have won the fourth match at Headingley.

They had won the opening match at Lord's by an innings when Gary Sobers scored 183 to support an innings of 119 by Eddie Barlow, but we had taken the second game almost as convincingly when winning by eight wickets at Trent Bridge. Basil D'Oliveira was the main architect of that victory when taking seven wickets in that match.

Back bounced the Rest of the World at Edgbaston by four wickets and then came the match we should have won – aided by injuries to Barry Richards and Rohan Kanhai. Rohan was handicapped in both innings and Barry did not bat in the first. He was hoping not to bat at all but found himself forced to go to the wicket when the Rest of the World stumbled to 183 for eight, needing 223 to win. Behind Barry there was only Lance Gibbs to come.

We all thought Barry should have been given out almost straight away. He played forward against Don Wilson, appeared to edge the ball on to his pad and then into the hands of silly mid-on. Our shout for a catch was turned down and Barry stayed with Mike Procter, the two South Africans seeing the Rest of the World to victory. Three-one down, our chance of glory had disappeared with that umpiring decision.

Gary, leading the Rest of the World side, was in his element that summer, revelling in the challenge provided by the company he kept, and back at his best. Over the last ten years I suppose most bowlers would put Gary at the top of their list of wanted men and his wicket always gave me an immense feeling of satisfaction, whether he had nought against his name as at the Oval in 1966 or 183 as at Lord's in 1970.

Yet, looking back over my career, I always rated taking the wicket of Seymour Nurse as a greater feat than dismissing Sobers. Nurse could be a brilliant and savage stroke-maker on his day, but could graft when necessary. Whereas Sobers – Rohan Kanhai and Clive Lloyd too – always gave me hope by the extravagance and richness of the stroke-play, I seldom had that same feeling of expectation when bowling to Nurse.

He may not have made the same impact on other people and will not be remembered for as long as many other West Indies batsmen for he appeared in only 29 Test matches. Yet his record speaks for itself. He had the misfortune to try to take over the West Indies middle order when Everton Weekes and Clyde Walcott retired from Test cricket. He averaged nearly 50.

Nurse was the second highest scorer against us on the 1966 West Indies tour to this country and Kanhai only just pipped him to that position when I toured the West Indies under Colin Cowdrey. He would probably have been remembered more in England if injury had not often kept him out of the great West Indies side under Sir Frank Worrell in 1963, although he still scored three centuries on that tour.

I had good reason to remember him when I came in for the last three Test matches in 1966. In my first game – the third Test – Nurse made 93 and 53 at Trent Bridge. In the next game he made 137 when sharing in a fifth-wicket partnership of 265 with Sobers at Headingley and at the Oval made up for a first innings duck by scoring 70 in the second innings when the West Indies were sliding towards their innings defeat.

He was always smiling, a very happy individual. A smile which developed into a laugh when he hooked me for six in Georgetown with the ball going straight over Alan Knott's head. He looked back down the wicket at me and laughed, a great big "pearly" laugh.

After Sobers, the player who caught the imagination in the Rest of the World series was South African all-rounder Eddie Barlow, who has now come to Derbyshire's aid. He was – and still is – a human dynamo of a player. A man for all seasons and situations who always seems to be in the thick of any battle playing his part whether it is with the bat, ball or simply as a fielder.

He possesses immense enthusiasm, tremendous confidence and just bubbles with energy, always pleading to be allowed to bowl by promising his captain that he will take a wicket when given the chance. He often succeeds, as at Headingley in 1970 when he did just this and came on to take four wickets in five balls during England's first innings.

The cold figures of 1970 illustrate his importance to that side for he finished the third highest run-scorer – behind Sobers and Clive Lloyd – the second highest wicket-taker – again behind Sobers – and also claimed ten catches. It was the one department of the game in which Sobers could not better him.

The series also produced two new players for England who were to prove their worth in Australia just a few months later. Brian Luckhurst emerged as an opening batsman playing in all five games and, right at the end, came Peter Lever. He was brought in for the final game at the Oval as the third fast bowler in support of Chris Old and myself and overshadowed both of us by finishing with seven for 83 in the first innings, figures which earned him his plane ticket to Australia.

Back with Sussex the season was almost a repeat of the previous one with just five victories to show for our efforts despite an improvement in our batting which resulted in a greater share of bonus points. It should have been a source of satisfaction yet it served only to increase our frustration.

Only two other sides gained more bonus points than we did yet we finished two places lower in the table than in 1968 when ninth. Once more we were below the half-way mark. Again the figures supported the arguments presented by the senior players for a number of years. Over the first two days we were a match for any side but still lacked the players and the necessary direction to finish off the operation on the third day. We were just not getting anywhere.

So far as the John Player League was concerned we were hopelessly out of touch with the demands of the game, finishing last for the second successive season. Failures in 40-over cricket, we still managed to reach the final of the 60-over Gillette Cup for the fourth time.

We had beaten Essex, Kent and Surrey for the right to meet Lancashire at Lord's. Once there, we seldom looked like making a fight of it. Our total of 184 – despite three men run out – was reasonable enough, but we never displayed the tactical awareness in the field to defend it as Lancashire strolled to victory by six wickets, with Harry Pilling the hero and man of the match with an undefeated 70.

Away from the actual playing side other incidents at the club were raising doubts in my mind about the direction Sussex cricket was taking. Like the time Tony Greig, Ken Suttle and myself attended a cricket dinner during the winter and sat opposite one of our committee members who ran the whole organisation.

As we took our seats he looked across at Tony Greig and said: "Ah, you must be Greig because you're so tall." Then he turned to me and said: "I recognise you because I've seen your picture in the newspapers" and finally he came to Ken Suttle and said: "That means you must be Ken Suttle because the three of you were coming."

What an insult. Kenny had been ever present in the Sussex side that summer and the previous season had established a remarkable run of 423 consecutive championship matches before being dropped. He had been one of the stalwarts of the club during the 1960s yet here was a committee member of Sussex unable to recognise him, who knew me only because of my picture in the newspapers and guessed at Tony Greig's identity purely because of his height. How could we have faith in the people running the club if this man represented the type of person who was being elected to office?

I have forgotten his name now but it would not surprise me if he were the man who caused a stir when he came to Hove soon after being elected to the committee.

He arrived at the top gate and asked the way to the committee room. By chance an established committee member happened to be entering the ground at the same time and offered to show the way.

Never having seen this new man before he was surprised to find he was on the committee.

They were walking around the top of the ground just after the scheduled start when the committee-man remarked to the newcomer: "I see Sussex are batting then."

"How do you know?" asked the newcomer.

"Well," came the reply, "that happens to be the opposition in the field and Oakman and Suttle are batting."

"I see," said the newcomer. "By the way, which one is Oakman."

Here was someone who could quite easily end up running the club yet he couldn't tell one Sussex player from another. Not even if they were Alan Oakman with his 6ft 5in lean frame topped by fair hair and Ken Suttle, chunky, dark-haired and some 10 inches shorter.

After hearing stories like these I couldn't wait to board that plane to Australia and immerse myself in the activities of England again to help clear Sussex from my mind.

1970–71: Australia. Crowds and management

AFTER READING the previous chapters it should come as no surprise to anybody that Ray Illingworth's leadership had my full support throughout the stormy 1970–71 tour of Australia. England won the series 2–0 to become the first side to reclaim the Ashes in Australia since that controversial "bodyline" explosion under Douglas Jardine's captaincy almost 40 years earlier.

I supported Ray when he defended me in the face of some peculiar judgements from Australian umpires, the details of which I will explain more fully later.

I supported him in that incident-packed final Test match in Sydney, when he led us off the field after I had been attacked by a spectator and the playing area at one end of the ground became littered with beer cans and bottles tossed by some of the crowd much the worse for drink. Drunkards have become a major problem on some Australian grounds.

I also supported Ray in the stand he took against the unco-operative attitudes of Australian officials and our own manager David Clark, now the chairman of Kent.

Ray flew to Australia determined he was going to return home a winner. He achieved his objective with a single-mindedness that had to be admired. He saw his hopes threatened when every major batsman went down injured at some time, and when he lost Alan Ward through injury before the Test series had got under way.

By the end of the second Test in Perth it was obvious to all that the management of the tour was split when Mr Clark made a statement to the Australian Press which criticised both Ray and Australian captain Bill Lawry for their approach in the first two games, both of which were drawn. In essence he said he would rather the Australians won the series than see a repetition of the cricket the first two Tests had produced. He also criticised the number of bouncers bowled. The first Ray knew of this was when an Australian journalist woke him about 6.30 in the morning seeking a comment. The rest of us knew nothing until we read it in the newspapers at the airport prior to our flight to Adelaide.

I concede that the cricket produced in those first two Tests was nothing to write home about. Nobody gets bored faster than I do (some people may have noticed) by games that lose their sense of purpose and just drift on waiting for time to be called, like a lonely drinker at the bar with nowhere to go.

Nobody likes them. Nobody gets involved in that type of game deliberately. But no right-minded cricketer is going to travel half-way around the world and hand the game to the opposition without a bitter struggle. Bill Lawry certainly was not the type of character to give the opposition anything, especially when all he had to do was draw the series to emerge as a "winner."

Let me say at once that nobody wanted the parting of the ways between management and ourselves but it was inevitable as a result of the manager's attitude. Perhaps, as a result, a greater effort is being made to ensure that tour managers and players are more of a like mind in the future. At the time Ray and I sat with the manager in the stands at Adelaide trying to put our point of view about his statement but, after an hour, we were no nearer a mutual understanding and just gave up.

The views of the English and Australian organising bodies are also far from harmonious. There's a tit-for-tat battle going on between them – "we played all the counties the last time in England so you must go up-country" and *vice versa* – without any regard for the players. A player feels he is just excess baggage, or at best a minion whose job is to wave the flag.

We came across an example of this in Australia later on the tour when arrangements were made to add an extra Test to the series, after the scheduled third Test in Melbourne had been washed out. This was in addition to the one-day limited over game which was hastily arranged when the Melbourne ground dried out, and despite the fact that we were playing six Tests anyway to allow Perth, the home of Western Australian cricket, to stage a Test for the first time.

We were not consulted about the extra Test match although Sir Cyril Hawker, then President of MCC, and "Gubby" Allen, MCC treasurer, were in Melbourne at the time to assist David Clark in discussions with the Australian authorities. The first we knew about it was when Sir Donald Bradman came into our dressing room and said: "It's very nice of you fellows to agree to play the extra game." It was hard enough that we should get the news; even worse that we had not been told by one of our own officials.

Our main concern about the extra match was that it could jeopardise our chance of winning the Ashes. Our injury rate was alarming, yet here we were being asked to commit ourselves to playing 20 days of Test cricket in the last 40 days of our stay in Australia.

That was a tough enough programme in itself without our other obligations – the matches already arranged between the Tests – plus the time spent travelling. As a result of the extra match I worked out that we had only one day free from cricket in those last six weeks in Australia apart from the rest days during the Test matches.

There was no suggestion that we should receive any extra payment for helping the Australian authorities to maintain their profits from the tour. Now this is not being mean or moody. This was an extra game over and above the agreement we had made when we accepted the terms for the tour. The players were making the sacrifice but there was no offer of compensation until the dinner before the fifth Test when we asked for more. Previously the majority of us had met in one of the hotel rooms and all but come out on strike about it.

Even then it took several weeks and repeated requests to David Clark to act on our behalf before we learned we were going to receive an extra £100. This was long after the Australian authorities announced they were paying their players extra money. If only we had been consulted in the first place I am sure much of the unpleasantness would not have arisen. That's all we want as professionals: a chance to be considered and consulted.

The whole scene for the Third Test in Melbourne was a circus from start to finish, a comic exhibition with the Melbourne authorities trying to get the Test match started when the umpires and the captains were totally agreed that the conditions were simply not fit. It was raining from the early morning on the first day, left off enough for Ray and Bill Lawry to toss up and then started again before there was any chance of getting on the field.

By lunchtime it was obvious that conditions were not going to be fit for play that day. They were worse on the second with the area surrounding the covers resembling a bog, yet still the Melbourne authorities were trying to insist there was a chance of a start being made. Ian Johnson, the former Australian Test player who is now secretary of the Melbourne Cricket Club, was particularly keen – and upset when the umpires and captains refused to consider the possibility.

On the first day I believe the Melbourne ground authorities made trouble for themselves by announcing – on more than one occasion – that play would start as soon as the rain stopped, thus encouraging people to come into the ground, many of them having travelled large distances from up-country outposts. The more people turned up in response to these announcements, the greater the attempt to get us to play, even when rain was still falling.

On the second day Ian Johnson went out to the middle to help remove the covers when he thought play should start – and promptly fell flat on his back when he lost his footing! To the credit of the umpires, they refused to be influenced by all the attempts to force them into a wrong decision. I think they were as amused by the antics of the Melbourne staff as we were. Not that we found the staff amusing on all occasions. They really were overtaken by a power complex during Test matches.

The gatemen in particular were savage and rude. They have had such a reputation for years and seemed determined to maintain the tradition by being as obstructive as possible. They refused to let a group of us in one day because we did not have a pass, even though we arrived in an official car and were wearing our full touring uniform. They even barred the way to Ian Redpath, the Victorian opening batsman, because he had forgotten his player's pass for a Test match. This was on his own home ground. How ridiculous can you get?

On another occasion Jack Hampshire and Ken Shuttleworth wanted a game of squash and tried to go through the pavilion to Ian Johnson's office for the key to the courts. They made it most of the way until an official barred their path and attempted to push them out as they tried to explain the purpose of their mission.

It was not as if they had anything to be proud of in Melbourne. The practice wickets they provided for us before the Test matches were a disgrace and we were forced to go in search of suitable nets on a school ground. They may have a huge concrete bowl of a stadium providing accommodation for 120,000 people, but there was nowhere for the players to dry their gear when they came off the field. And it needs drying after a couple of hours on the field in temperatures around the the three figure mark. No whitening was provided either for cleaning of boots or pads. These things are not much to ask for but sadly are often unavailable on grounds the world over.

Despite the happenings in Sydney during the final Test, I placed the Melbourne crowd top of the nastiness league. Gluttons for sport they demanded not one but two pounds of flesh. They lacked humour, wit and variation. "Have a go, yer mug" ceased to have any meaning when you'd heard it for the 300th time in a day. They had been raised on the Australian Rules, a tough mixture of football and rugby and seemed to demand their "blood" from cricket as well. They reminded me of the bloodthirsty crowds depicted in Hollywood biblical epics, calling for more when the Christians were thrown to the lions.

It's a great pity for I'm all in favour of crowd participation. I do not believe in cricket being played in a vacuum, unlike one Sussex secretary who announced over the tannoy system at Hove one day that talking was only permitted between overs! To me part of the appeal of one-day cricket in England is the bubble and enthusiasm of the crowd – even when it is having a go at me.

John Edrich certainly found spectator-participation in Brisbane. He chased one of many balls around the boundary during Keith Stackpole's onslaught and just failed to cut it off. As he bent down to pick it up a chap in the front row reflectively called out: "You're following in your cousin's footsteps you know. I was sitting here 25 years ago and he spent all day chasing the ball along the same piece of grass. He didn't stop it much either."

Perhaps the worst feature of a section of the Melbourne crowd is their drunken brawling. Policemen told me they would like to see it curtailed but added they were powerless to act because they received such little backing from the ground authorities. Fights are continuous but many people are allowed to get away with punch-drunk activities for which they would be arrested outside the ground. No one would suggest stopping an Australian drinking. That would be like taking air from his lungs, but there is room for moderation.

Annoying as the events were in Melbourne when the third Test was washed out I should add that many of the irritations on the tour came from our side. In Brisbane, for instance, we asked David Clark for car park passes to get into the ground for the Test match as several of us had been loaned cars by firms or friends for our stay in the city. We were all taken aback when Mr Clark told us we would have to pay the 20c car parking fee like the spectators, just as he'd been doing during the Queensland game. I know of one car that got in for nothing.

The meal allowance was another source of annoyance. Often too low to provide us with a decent meal, it forced us to dip into our own pockets. The rate had been fixed without taking into consideration the relative prices of hotels. Then there was the question of dress, when we were required to be done up to the nines with shirt, tie and blazer in a temperature of 90 degrees for a four-hour plane trip. The countless round of official receptions which are the bugbear of any touring party provided yet another irritation – many were completely unnecessary and the guests attended because it was the "done thing" rather than through any genuine interest.

Far too many functions were accepted by the MCC management and I take two examples from my diary of that tour to show why they were cursed by the players. After the first Test in Brisbane we were booked on an early flight – needing a seven a.m. getaway from our hotel – for our journey to Perth across the other side of Australia and the setting for the second Test.

The journey took us over eight hours and led straight to a cocktail party that evening. The next morning we had nets followed by an official reception at lunchtime in the centre of the city, more nets in the afternoon, a team meeting at five o'clock and then on to a cocktail party in the evening.

On another occasion we arrived in Hobart, droppped our bags at the hotel, turned the cars around and went off to the British High Commission to be greeted by just four people.

On the question of dress I'm not a tie man myself. I do not believe a tie is essential or that a person looks smart or is a good bloke just because he is wearing one. Casual clothes can look just as neat. Certainly MCC have taken that view on some tours. In the West Indies in 1968 we were all fitted out with identical white shirts with dark blue collars for travelling from island to island and for many official functions. Why could the same not apply in Australia or India?

Such things helped to strain the relationship between Ray and the manager. Obviously I had my differences with David Clark on those matters also. But my once-and-for-all clash with him came before the state game in Perth.

To a large extent Ray left the question of my fitness to me. Occasionally he would come up and ask me to have a bowl flat out in the nets so that he could have a look but, by then, he recognised that I knew what was needed from me and trusted me to adjust my programme and thinking to be at a peak when required during the Test matches. This was something I appreciated.

Immediately before Perth I had bowled more than 50 overs during the drawn first Test taking four wickets in a spell in the Australian first innings when they slumped from a lofty 418 for four to 433 all out. As a result of this performance I was rested for the state match against Western Australia, although I still had to report for the net session on the morning of the game.

I admit I did not feel like bowling and delivered a couple with my left arm, at which Mr Clark snapped at me: "bowl properly." So I sent down a couple of slowish right-arm deliveries, which was a warming up process as my back was pretty stiff. He didn't wait to see any further development in my bowling but stormed off. Later, when the boys went out to field, he called me back into the dressing room where he lost his temper in a five-minute outburst.

Three or four times I tried to interrupt the flow with a "but manager" in order to put my viewpoint, as he accused me of not pulling my weight, and of not bowling enough or properly. In the end I had to wait until he had run out of words before I could reply that I was fed up with being treated like a schoolboy. I had got that far without his help and I knew exactly what was required of me.

I told him that as far as my "good conduct" money was concerned he could swallow it.

The exchange was very heated before I went back to the nets and bowled to Jack Hampshire and Basil D'Oliveira who both wanted batting practice. After this, feeling completely dismayed with the management I went "walk about" as the Australians say. I just had to get away from the cricket atmosphere for 24 hours to ease the frustration and recapture some zest and enthusiasm, so I broke bounds and went off down the Western Australia coast to spend the night at the home of a friend.

To be completely fair to David Clark, he had some basis for an argument if it is conceded that everybody is alike. One or two of the boys, particularly Peter Lever, had a few grumbles about me after we had taken a hammering from the South Australian batsmen, especially Barry Richards, who was spending a season there and took us for a double century. That was our first meeting with him; he scored a century the second time also.

My attitude was that we were in Australia to win the Test matches, the state games being secondary and useful for match practice and as a means of keeping in trim. I saw no point in bursting myself to score a point over Barry. It was not a case of not trying, but I wasn't going to burn myself out just to get his scalp especially early on in the tour. Bowling figures had long since lost their meaning to me after my experiences with Sussex, when I had been required to bowl on all sorts of surfaces.

Ray quickly learned of these grumbles and tackled me about them. He said he recognised that I knew exactly what I was doing but suggested that I should also take into consideration the thinking of the other bowlers. Although my Test place was pretty certain, Peter Lever, Ken Shuttleworth, Alan Ward and the others were fighting for their opportunity and were relying on good returns from these state games in order to push their claims.

He explained it in reasonable terms and I saw his point. It must have been a little exasperating for the others, particularly Peter Lever who, like David Brown, has put everything into his bowling to extract the maximum benefit at the other end. It was not so much a question of me having to perk up my bowling but to be a little more alive in the field to support the other bowlers.

It was not all moan. Far from it. From the moment Ray took charge and most of the party took one step sideways to line up behind him, the tour went smoothly enough. One has only to glance at the results from Perth onwards to see the dramatic change. We arrived in Brisbane for the first Test as outsiders after a disappointing run of performances while we were adjusting to the conditions. From the second Test in Perth onwards we became the favourites and always looked capable of snatching the Ashes back.

There were many chuckles as well. I had one in Melbourne when attempts to run a smear campaign against me in a newspaper came unstuck. I was accused of cheating by repeatedly picking the seam. The story was supported by exclusive pictures which, it was claimed, showed me picking the seam as I walked back to my mark, my body supposedly concealing my cheating activities from the umpires. It was quite a splash.

What the newspaper men did not realise was that I knew they were attempting to "make" this story. I saw the photographer snapping away with his camera – there could be no other reason for taking photographs at that moment – and I played up to him by pretending to run my thumb nail under the seam and do all sorts of nasty things to the ball.

They also failed to realise that it is impossible to pick the seam on a Kookaburra ball as it hardly has one. If I do appear to be messing about with the ball I can assure you my activities are perfectly innocent, just cleaning out the earth from the seam where it has pitched and repairing the "bruises" where the bat has hit the shiny side. Something totally different.

The celebrations after our first victory in Sydney took some beating for laughs as well. They started, naturally, with champagne in the England dressing room, more back in the hotel and then we celebrated at any door that would open to our knock.

Nobody enjoys victory more than Basil D'Oliveira and I shall never forget him in Sydney after we had won that Test. Nobody was more proud of the team's performance.

I am surprised that Basil still has a forefinger on his right hand the number of times he stabbed it into the chest of complete strangers that night and told them "we stuffed you." It didn't matter who they were, where they came from or what they were, they all received the same treatment. Greek immigrants, Italian immigrants, Spanish immigrants, waiters, doormen, businessmen, guests, hosts, Australians, Englishmen, cricket lovers, non-cricket fans were left in no doubt by Bas that they had all "been stuffed."

I also had a disappointment that night. Somewhere along the line I was presented with a large and very unusually shaped wine bottle which I thought would make an ideal base for a table lamp. I protected this souvenir with my life from party to party until dawn was breaking and my final taxi ride back to the hotel. Not until I reached my room did I remember that I had left it in the back of the cab never to be seen again. It is probably now decorating some table in a Sydney suburb.

1970–71: Bitter rows with Umpire Rowan

SO FAR I have deliberately refrained from mentioning the name of Lou Rowan, the Brisbane detective who doubled as an umpire in his spare time. It is not an oversight. In any attempt to set down my cricketing adventures, Rowan needs a chapter to himself, for he highlights a world-wide problem of amateur umpires with no first-class playing experience making decisions which can change the whole course of a series.

In 15 seasons of first-class cricket, performing in front of umpires all over the cricket-playing world, I can safely say that I have never come across another umpire so full of his own importance, so stubborn, lacking in humour, unreasonable and utterly unable to distinguish between a delivery short of a length which rises around the height of the rib cage and a genuine bouncer which goes through head high, as Lou Rowan.

I write as I found Rowan on that 1970–71 tour of Australia and not what may have gone before. I have no wish to question the reputation he had gained over previous seasons when he was regarded as one of Australia's top officials. But, after my experiences, I found myself agreeing with one critic, who had watched Rowan in action many times, when he came to the conclusion that Rowan had undone many of the good things in his umpiring life by staying on for one tour too many.

Perhaps the pressure told on him during the 1970–71 tour when he found himself cast in the role of Australia's senior umpire for the first time in his life. Until then he had lived in the shadow of Col Eager, the Adelaide umpire who gained a world-wide reputation as one of the game's outstanding officials during the 1960s. Sadly – so far as we were concerned – Eager announced his retirement from Test cricket while we were still engaged on our warm-up tour of Australia before the opening Test match.

Whatever the reason for Rowan's obvious decline as a Test umpire it resulted in the two of us exchanging words on more than one occasion, culminating in the crowd scenes during the final game at Sydney which prompted Ray Illingworth to lead us off the field for our own protection and safety. These exchanges Rowan rushed into print in the most inventive way in his book "The Umpire's Story" (Jack Pollard, Sydney, 1972), despite his statement at the end of the tour when he said: "Because of my great love for cricket and the respect I have for many closely associated with it, I have no comment to make. I will not join the group at any wailing wall." As it turned out he wasn't long in crying.

I say he rushed into print in a most inventive way for most of his detailed and reported exchanges with both myself and Ray Illingworth are written in a language with which I am not familiar.

For instance he quotes Ray saying to him after he had warned me at Sydney: "This is not — — fair! You can't — — well caution him. That's the only bouncer he's bowled. — — hell."

Later he reports a remark of mine as being: "You're a — — cheat. Whose — — side are you on anyway?" There are several other exchanges reported in a like manner. I swear now and again but this . . .

I can only marvel, too, at Rowan's memory in recalling the exact words used on each occasion spread over a three-month period taking in six Test matches. He has presented them as a strict report of what was said at the time which must take some doing, even with a notebook and pencil at the ready during each interval.

These examples confirmed the suspicions of what I might find inside when I saw the front jacket of the book, which consisted of a coloured photograph of a spectator at Sydney standing up and reaching out with his right hand over the boundary picket fence grabbing my left shirt sleeve. Yet on the back is posed the question: "Was John Snow actually grabbed by a spectator who objected to Snow flattening an Australian batsman?"

A quick glance at the start of the third chapter is also rather illuminating, showing Rowan has a basic lack of tactical knowledge of cricket despite his many years standing in the middle.

He writes that whenever possible Ray bowled me from the end opposite to the one at which he was standing because we could not overcome his attitude towards intimidatory bowling. This is ridiculous.

There was only one thing Ray and I took into consideration when deciding from which end I should open the attack, and that was the direction of the wind. As the recognised fast bowler I had the wind at my back whenever possible to help my pace. I switched ends only if a patch appeared on the wicket that I could exploit. Ask Peter Lever, who was my most regular opening partner on that tour. He bowled uphill and into the wind enough to remember that fact.

Yet the passage I find most revealing of all comes when Rowan recalls how he first came across us on that 1970–71 tour when we played against a Queensland Country XI in a little town called Warwick soon after our arrival in the state. Rowan had been speaking at a dinner in the town the night before and stayed over to watch the day's play having already been informed that he was officiating in the first Test in his home town of Brisbane.

Rowan reports remarks I am alleged to have made to local umpire Bill Priem – there are those double blank swear words again – after I had been no-balled for overstepping and then continues:

> 'A heavy thunderstorm broke at the end of the day. The visitors returned to George Andrew's hotel and after dinner, in a hurry to get back to Brisbane, they decided to brave the heavy rain in order to board their bus which was parked in front of the hotel.
>
> 'This involved crossing a wet footpath, stepping into or across a gutter, then taking a stride into the bus.
>
> 'None of them was aware that the gutter was about a foot deep and then was running a banker with rain water. Bill Priem and I, watching from an upstairs verandah, decided not to spoil the fun by warning them of the gutter. So we had a laugh to see them crossing the wet footpath, stepping gingerly to try to keep their feet dry, then into the gutter in which the water came halfway up their knees.
>
> 'Perhaps it was a little perverse of us not to have told them to avoid the water-filled gutter but already I had the feeling that I should enjoy as many laughs as possible at the expense of these fellows while the opportunity was there.'

If that is not sick I don't know what is.

I found it astonishing not only as an insight into the mind of Mr Rowan, but that he should make such an admission while he was trying to convince the cricketing world that all the right was on his side in his decision-making during the series.

In our dealings with an umpire with that outlook it is hardly surprising that Ray and I found ourselves simmering with frustration when trying to talk and explain matters to him on the field. Or that we both ended up on the carpet – along with Geoff Boycott – in front of the then MCC secretary Billy Griffith on our return to England to explain certain events out in the middle.

I had no knowledge of Rowan before I came across him for the first time in the match against Queensland immediately before the first Test. No set feelings about him at all, even after his blunder on the opening day of that first Test which saw Australia's opening batsman Keith Stackpole escape a run-out decision when he was on 18 and go on to make a career best 207. Angry about the decision, of course. Upset with the umpiring, yes. But not with Rowan as a person. He was just a name to me at the time.

We were all angry, especially Geoff Boycott who actually did the fielding and threw down the wicket at the bowler's end when Stackpole attempted to drive and dashed for the single. And especially Derek Underwood who had raced to the wicket to take the return. Both were certain that Stackpole was out of his crease when the wicket was broken. Rowan gave Stackpole the benefit of the doubt, a decision that was to cost us almost 200 runs as Australia made 433 in their first innings, giving them a springboard for a possible victory. If the decision had gone our way we might have been in the driving seat for Australia had already lost Bill Lawry at the time, caught behind hooking against me.

One snappy cameraman confirmed the impressions of Boycott and Underwood. Before the day's play had finished the newspapers were already splashing a picture showing that Stackpole's bat was outside the return crease at the time the wicket was broken. By the next morning some of the Australian papers were describing Rowan's decision as one of the worst in cricket history, and it was the main topic of controversy on all cricket radio and television broadcasts.

It would take an extraordinary man to be able to put all that fuss behind him and wipe it from his mind, and I am convinced that the memory of that mistaken decision remained with Rowan for the rest of the tour.

There is no doubt that we began to question Rowan's competence from that moment, having already encountered one or two strange umpiring decisions on our way to Brisbane. One in particular involved me, when I was no-balled 17 times by umpire Ron Joseph in the state game against South Australia at Adelaide. If I remember correctly, they were all for over-stepping.

I have no hesitation in saying that I was probably guilty on a few of those occasions. I could see that from my own footmarks. But there were several other times when I knew I had cut the line as the law permits. When this happened more than once I asked Joseph for an explanation and he astonished me by saying that he was no-balling me because I was delivering off my left toes with my heel in the air and therefore not cutting the line. It is a physical impossibility for me to bowl like this with my action and I wasn't sure whether to laugh or cry. I just asked Joseph if he'd brought his coat of many colours with him.

My first real brush with Rowan came towards the end of the second Test match in Perth, a match marked by a fighting 171 from Ian Redpath and a sparkling century by Greg Chappell on his Test debut, as Australia reached 440 in reply to our 397, in which Brian Luckhurst reached three figures.

Another century, this time by John Edrich, enabled Ray to declare our second innings and set Australia 248 to win with time for about 32 eight-ball overs. A faint chance for Australia to go ahead in the series if they accepted the challenge or for us if we could make a quick breakthrough.

Although not as fast as some Perth wickets have been, the wicket still had a little pace and lift in it on the last day and I tried to make life as difficult as possible by bowling a number of deliveries just short of a length and making them rise up between hip and shoulder high. Both opening batsmen Bill Lawry and Keith Stackpole had been dismissed off similar deliveries in the first innings and Ian Chappell – in those days – and Doug Walters possessed little idea of how to counter deliveries rising chest high.

It was then that I ran into trouble with Rowan. Simply on a matter of interpretation. He says in his book that at one time he counted as many as five bouncers or bumpers in an over when he was standing at square leg, and complained I sent down many more when I bowled from his end before he stepped in with a warning.

They weren't bouncers. Not the vast majority of them. I did bowl the odd one just to have an unsettling effect on the batsmen or perhaps tempt them into a mishook. I wasn't wasting energy by bowling them all the time. My aim was to bowl the ball just short of a length aiming to get it up around chest high.

Bowled properly this is one of the most difficult deliveries for a batsman to counter. It is not short enough for him to hook. Yet it is just a shade too high for him to get his bat up and on top of it in an attempt to block it successfully. In an effort to play the ball and control it, the batsman has to tuck himself up in an awkward position and, in doing so, offers the chance of finding the edge of the bat or the glove.

The batsmen were in difficulties. They simply were not good enough at that stage to play that delivery and I suspect that Rowan confused their problems with intimidatory bowling, even though the deliveries were not aimed for the head or going through head high.

Twice Rowan warned me for intimidatory bowling and twice I told him he could not possibly interpret those deliveries as being a threat to the batsman's physical well-being. It was after the second remark that he called over Ray and issued an official warning which meant that after one further warning I would be banned from bowling for the rest of the match.

As it happened time was running out and Ray had already told me it was to be my last over. I had one ball left and in my frustration I pitched it short so that it went through just over the batsman's head. I turned to Rowan and said: "Now that's a bouncer for you" before walking off to my fielding position.

This first real clash between us aroused deeper suspicions inside me about his competence, particularly after he had turned down two leg-before appeals against Stackpole in the first innings when he had been struck on the leg right in front of the wicket, once by Shuttleworth and once by Lever. In fact the complete scorecard of the tour makes interesting reading on the question of leg before dismissals. Australia had five of their shouts rewarded. We never got one in six full Test matches. Remarkable really.

It is not often in Australia that the atmospheric conditions encourage swing and there is little deviation off the wicket. Sydney is an exception and it was on this ground that we won the Ashes with victories in the fourth and seventh Tests.

The Sydney wicket did offer some encouragement, with Johnny Gleeson and Ashley Mallett taking eight wickets between them in our first innings of 332 in the fourth Test, while Derek Underwood took four in helping to limit the Australian reply to 236, giving us a first innings lead of 96.

With Geoff Boycott scoring a magnificent 142 not out in our second innings of 319 for five, Ray was able to declare, setting Australia 416 to win and leaving us with plenty of time to bowl them out. By this time a patch had appeared on about a good length at one end of the wicket which made Geoff's innings an even more memorable feat, for the patch seldom bothered him. The Australians were in all kinds of trouble when they began their task.

The patch was just on a right length for me to exploit and with the full co-operation of the fielders who took some marvellous catches, I finished with seven for 40 from my eighteen eight-ball overs leaving Australia all out for 116 and England home by 299 runs. The reclamation of the Ashes was one step nearer.

In fact I accounted for eight of the batsmen, for poor Graham McKenzie was struck a nasty blow in the face from a ball which rose viciously from the worn ground and was unable to bat again.

The fifth Test in Melbourne – the one rearranged to make up for the washed out scheduled third Test – was a bore from start to finish on a wicket which got better and better. I was still to run into trouble for intimidatory bowling however.

This time the warning came from umpire Max O'Connell who was standing in his first Test. Like Rowan I thought he was being harsh but there was an altogether different reaction when Ray and I spoke to O'Connell. We felt he was human.

He didn't start the match too well. He took the first over, which I bowled, and off the last ball Stackpole flashed outside the off stump to give Alan Knott an easy catch behind. By this time however Max was already walking towards square leg ready for the next over and missed the incident. In his nervousness he had called "over" as I delivered the ball and started to turn away almost before Stackpole played his stroke. He had no alternative but to turn down the appeal giving Stackpole yet another life on the tour. Whenever I've seen Max on my return to Australia we've had a laugh about it. I could quite understand his actions which illustrate the pressure umpires are also under in a Test.

Max's intimidatory warning came in the Australian second innings after I'd bowled one or two shortish deliveries against Doug Walters. My objection on this occasion was hinged on the fact that Australian fast bowler Alan "Froggy" Thomson had bowled a large number of bouncers at us in our first innings without once receiving a warning. Not short of a length deliveries, but ones that pitched half way down the track and went through above head high. He bowled six bouncers at Ray Illingworth in one over without being spoken to. They were harmless efforts but it showed a lack of consistency when he could bowl bouncers without a word while I was warned for bowling balls chest high.

The main controversy of the sixth Test in Adelaide centred around Ray's decision not to enforce the follow-on after we had scored 470 in our first innings and Australia had been bowled out for 235. Peter Lever was largely responsible for their total with four wickets for 49. He missed the first Test of the series, had been the first change in the next two, first behind Ken Shuttleworth and then Bob Willis, but he opened the attack with me in the fifth Test. He bowled well in Adelaide and thoroughly deserved his wickets, while I was beginning to feel the strain, the sixth Test following on immediately from the Melbourne game.

This was one of the major factors behind Ray's decision not to ask the Australians to bat again. Before making his decision he consulted both Peter Lever and myself and we admitted that we were tired. If we had been forced to bowl again immediately we couldn't promise to keep going at top pace for very long. In addition Lever was feeling a shoulder strain and I had been suffering with my old back problem before the match and had been forced to have it stretched. It was still tender. The wicket was also plumb and we did not think the Australians could possibly bat so badly a second time around.

There were still two days to go plus an hour of the third day when Ray had to make his decision. The last thing he wanted was for the Australians to score freely and put us under pressure to survive the greater part of the last day. There was also the possibility of the wicket breaking up a little and being awkward on the last day when we would have to bat after more then three days in the field.

The final consideration was the coming last Test in Sydney on the wicket most likely to produce a result. By now Ray had judged the mood and feeling of the Australians and was convinced we would win. But he still wanted Bob Willis, Peter Lever and myself completely rested and fresh for the final assault.

1970–71: Ashes triumph in Sydney

THE ONE person Ray didn't bargain for being without in Sydney for the final Test match was Geoff Boycott, who had been sent reeling out of the game a few days beforehand when he had his left arm broken by a rising delivery from Graham McKenzie in a one-day match played on a wet wicket.

Neither did he bargain for losing me soon after the start of Australia's second innings when I smashed the little finger on my right hand into the boundary fence when going for a hook by Keith Stackpole off Peter Lever, the ball sailing over the long leg boundary. That put me out of the most vital session of the series when Australia were chasing 223 to win and so draw the series.

However, the injury didn't come early enough to prevent one last heated exchange with Rowan, or Ray being forced to take us from the field after a shower of beer cans and bottles had sailed over the fence and one spectator had tried to clobber me. I believe Rowan's attitude sparked the incident.

Let me set the scene. Leading Australia for the first time in place of the sacked Bill Lawry, Ian Chappell had won the toss and asked us to bat on a damp wicket offering considerable help to the bowlers. We were bowled out for 184, more runs we would have got if the Australian bowlers had used the wicket properly. Fortunately for us they had made a selection blunder by dropping Graham McKenzie. He might well have proved a match winner for the Australians in those conditions.

Small though our total may have appeared it began to look larger than it was in the eyes of the Australians by the close of that first day when Knotty took a brilliant catch off Lever's bowling to dismiss Eastwood and I bowled Stackpole comprehensively. They finished on 13 for two and far from happy.

The explosion happened on the second day after Australia had clawed their way into a lead at 195 for seven, with Redpath the main architect, playing well for his 59 runs, while Walters scratched around for 42 during which he was given a life by another blunder by Rowan.

In going down the track against Underwood, he was beaten by the flight with the ball striking his foot before Knotty grabbed it and whipped off the bails. Walters, bat in air, was still well out of his crease but Rowan, at square leg, turned down the shout. It was an astonishing decision. I was fielding at square leg just a yard or so from Rowan and saw the incident clearly. When I asked Rowan why he had turned down the appeal he said he gave Walters the benefit of the doubt. There was no shadow of doubt about it.

Fortunately it didn't prove expensive this time. Walters added only one more run before he was again beaten by Underwood's flight and stumped leaving Greg Chappell as the only threat, with much depending on how long the tail enders could stay with him.

There was not long to go when I was brought back into the attack with the new ball, Australian leg spinner Terry Jenner now partnering Greg Chappell. Although batting at number nine Jenner is no mug with the bat. He had made a number of useful scores for South Australia and was beginning to settle in with Chappell, the pair of them having added 17 to take Australia ahead.

I decided to bowl him a shortish delivery just to remind him he could not go safely on the front foot. It was not a bouncer and would not have got above rib high if Jenner had not ducked into it, the ball catching him on the head. Down he went. When he returned from hospital he admitted it was his fault entirely.

Rowan obviously thought otherwise. He warned me for intimidatory bowling. I couldn't believe it.

I admit quite openly that I lost my temper with that warning. There was absolutely no justification for it and I'm sure it inflamed the situation. Partly because he issued it but largely as a result of the way he issued it.

In his account of the incident in his book Rowan writes:

> 'I was determined not to place myself in a position where anyone could justly accuse me of any form of provocation. This is why I waited until Snow was on his way back to resume bowling before making any attempt to advise him on the manner of his bowling.'

Surely this was the worst thing he could have done. If he had any objection to my delivery and wanted to say something to me it could have been done quietly and unobtrusively while we were standing around waiting for Jenner to be treated and helped off the ground. That was a break in the play when the attention of the crowd was focused on Jenner and away from me for a moment.

The crowd was upset by the incident in seeing one of their own players injured with the match in such a delicate state. I was upset, too. I do not like hitting people. Even Australians. But with Jenner's removal from the field, the crowd was beginning to settle down again, two or three minutes having elapsed since Jenner was hit. This was the moment Rowan chose to make his stand. When the whole crowd could see what he was doing. If that wasn't a provocative act, what was?

With the exchange of words between us Ray naturally came over to see what was going on and was equally staggered to discover I had received a warning. He, too, protested that Rowan was wrong to act after just one shortish pitched delivery in the over and told Rowan he would be making an official complaint to the Australian Board of Control at the end of the day's play. I accept that we were wrong to argue on the field but having taken so much from Rowan during the tour frustration boiled over at that moment.

The booing started the moment I walked back to my mark to bowl the last ball of the over to Dennis Lillee who had replaced Jenner. A few beer cans came over too, but not enough to worry about at that stage. I was still upset when I bowled the ball down the leg side before snatching my cap from Rowan's hand and walking back to my fielding position at long leg.

The beer cans had increased now and I was still short of my position when Ray called me back into the middle and asked for the cans to be cleared. Once that was done I again started to walk to the boundary and was nearing the fence when some lads in the crowd reached out to shake me by the hand. The boos were echoing around the ground but there was a fair amount of sympathetic applause coming from some spectators as well.

At first I started to acknowledge the handshakes until I spotted a large fellow in the front row reaching out for me. I thought better of the handshakes and turned to face the field of play when this fellow grabbed my shirt sleeve and started to tug me towards the fence. He had grabbed me with his right hand but it was his free left hand I was worried about. I thought about striking out myself until I realised he was drunk, but in any case it would have been a stupid thing to do.

Fortunately the people who wanted to shake my hand realised what was happening and grabbed the drunk, enabling me to get away before he pulled me over the fence, but his action had sparked a revival of the beer can and bottle throwing. Cans and bottles were flying past me from all directions until I managed to get out of range, turning round to look at the crowd again. I waved at them as if saying, okay get on with it if you must. Not inviting them to fight as some people suggested. I was still looking at them, waiting for them to quieten down when Bob Willis came charging up and told me Ray was taking us off the field. I needed no second invitation to join him.

It was the only sensible thing to do as anybody who has experienced crowd scenes in the West Indies and Pakistan will recognise. It's the best way of bringing people to their senses. With the cans on the field – some of them with beer in – there was no question of play restarting immediately and to have remained we would have only been presenting the drunken element in the crowd with a target. Remove the target and there is no point in throwing anything. I would have thought Rowan would have recognised this especially as he was a policeman.

Despite all that has been written Ray was perfectly calm at that moment and in control of himself. Not until he reached the dressing room did his anger boil over and only then when the manager David Clark literally tried to push us back out onto the field. At that Ray went white with rage and suggested it was about time the manager looked after our interests and the safety of the players instead of siding with the Australians. Ray explained he wanted an announcement made that the team would return as soon as the playing area had been cleared and told the same to the umpires and Alan Barnes, secretary of the Australian Board of Control, when they appeared in the dressing room with a warning that the game would be awarded to the Australians if we did not return.

By the time we did return the field had been cleared, and the police had moved in to arrest the trouble-makers and clear out the drunkards. Not before one of the sight-screen attendants had been carted off to hospital after being hit on the head by a can of beer. I shall always remain convinced that our action in going off helped restore sanity faster than had we stayed.

My last act in that Test came on the fourth day. I had bowled only a couple of overs in the Australian second innings for the wicket of Eastwood. Then came Stackpole's heave against Peter Lever, my crash into the fence and off to hospital I went. Strangely enough the injury brought relief because for the first time in five months I relaxed as the pre-operation drugs took effect and I moved into another world. Nevertheless when I came round at about eight in the evening I was still greatly concerned about what was happening, and convinced that the game was still in progress insisted on asking the score every five minutes!

Back at the ground, however, Rowan still had a part to play which might have proved decisive. Keith Stackpole was only 13 when he went to drive Peter Lever, played down the wrong line and edged the ball behind for Knotty to take a catch. The boys told me afterwards the snick was so distinct, the deviation so great that they were absolutely stunned when Rowan turned down the appeal, allowing Stackpole to stay for another 54 runs before he was bowled by Ray. With his wicket went Australia's hopes and the Ashes were on their way back to England.

We triumphed despite the almost crippling run of injuries, which meant that many batsmen did not have the chance to play themselves into form before they suddenly found themselves pitchforked into the Test team. Despite the parting of the ways between the team and the manager. And despite the interference of Rowan, who was involved in five controversial "not out" decisions on the tour, four of them involving Stackpole. Wisely, in my opinion, he decided to retire from standing in international cricket at the end of the following season.

Perhaps the most amazing part of the whole Rowan episode was that he remained convinced he was right even when the other umpires did not support him. For the majority of the Tests in that series Rowan was partnered by Tom Brooks who was standing in a series for the first time following the retirement of Col Eager. I found Brooks, like O'Connell, a very reasonable and fair man, even if I did not always agree with him.

Brooks would have no part of Rowan's stand against me as Rowan admits. During the second Test at Perth, when Rowan first warned me for intimidatory bowling, he tried to discuss the issue with Brooks but failed. Rowan writes in his book:

> 'At intervals in this match I tried to get Tom Brooks's views on intimidatory bowling, the persistent bowling of fast, short-pitched balls at the batsman. We did not agree on the matter, but of course, I was aware that Tom was himself a fast bowler formerly. He said he believed fast bowlers must be allowed to do this.'

The Australians had helped us to win that last Test match by dropping Bill Lawry, ending his international career. Bill had been captain in the first six Test matches and led the side like he approached an innings at the crease – full of caution in a low key style and unwilling to take the slighest risk.

The side undoubtedly benefited by the change of captaincy, with Ian Chappell injecting a fresh approach, a more aggressive and inspirational type of leadership which improved team spirit. At the same time the side lost something by the absence of Lawry and he would have proved a major obstacle on that Sydney wicket if he had been playing. He might even have seen them through.

He always had to be got out and even if you managed to knock all three stumps over he still stayed at the crease a moment looking round for some excuse to continue batting before reluctantly starting his walk back to the dressing room. He was an exceptional judge of exactly where his off stump was which meant he could ignore deliveries 99 of 100 batsmen would have played.

Stubborn as Lawry was I have rated his Victorian partner Ian Redpath as the overseas player I liked bowling to least of all. He was what I term a real nuisance batsman.

In 1968 over in England he had a lean time with the bat in the Test series, but soon discovered his limitations and played within them. The West Indies certainly found him very difficult to remove on their 1975–76 tour of Australia, even with a battery of fast bowlers such as Andy Roberts, Michael Holding, Keith Boyce and Bernard Julien. I found him equally stubborn in 1970–71 when he batted in the middle order, and he generally did well against Mike Denness' side four years later when he played as an opening batsman following the retirement of Keith Stackpole.

Perhaps the most annoying feature of Ian as far as I was concerned was his almost saintly refusal to fall to any temptation put his way. Where the occasional bouncer and short of a length delivery caused a flutter in the hearts of most Australians in 1970–71, Ian remained completely unruffled by it all, at least on the outside.

He was just not interested in the bouncer, never had any intention of playing it however inviting it may have looked at the time. Instead he ducked and swayed out of the way rather in the way Alan Knott leaves them alone although with not quite the same exaggerated motion. He could play the short-of-a-length ball, too, having the height and the footwork to cope, so that he was seldom tucked up in an awkward position.

I found him a very straight player with a good technique, a superb judge of the ball and its line and a player who never flashed the bat around against fast bowling. It took a very good ball to find the edge of his bat. I thought he was a very useful player for the Australians to have around. The insurance type, able to keep one end going while the player at the other end produced the crowd-pleasing strokes.

During the 1970–71 tour I managed to take his wicket only three times but picked up another 28 and for that opportunity I must pay a tribute to Ray Illingworth for his handling of the side, the support of the other fast bowlers Peter Lever, Ken Shuttleworth and Bob Willis for the uncomplaining way they let me have the best of the conditions, and the superb form of Alan Knott, then unquestionably the best wicket keeper in the world.

Small, perky, with his elfin-like face, Alan is an action man – even when nothing is happening. Any lull will see him going through his routine of exercises aimed at keeping his joints supple and his mind alert ready to take a catch off the last ball of a tiring six-hour day just as nimbly as he would off the first.

Those exercises are not just confined to the field either. He can be murder to share a room with as Peter Lever found in Australia. One morning he woke at six to discover Knotty running up and down the corridor before starting a washing and brushing routine which took almost two hours to complete before he was ready to meet the outside world. He's a fanatic over his food, eating only specially selected health foods, but he's still a joy to have around. It makes a tremendous difference to a bowler knowing there is Knotty behind the wicket, where the vast majority of edges and snicks are going to be picked up in his remarkable pair of safe hands. It makes a great difference to the side as a whole having somebody there in whom they have 100 per cent confidence.

Bob Willis was a staggering success, considering he had little first-class experience behind him when he was whisked from England and the Surrey second eleven as a replacement for the injured Alan Ward. Not only in his bowling and fielding but in the remarkable way he settled down to become a member of the touring party. His rendering of "Barnacle Bill the Sailor" was a riot and became his party piece.

The one sadness among the players concerned Colin Cowdrey, who never really came to terms with the trip after his hesitation in accepting the invitation to tour under Ray's leadership. Not getting the captaincy was a terrible disappointment to him. Ray and he didn't hit it off, and he didn't agree with the attitudes of the majority of us regarding the manager and the tour as a whole, so that by the end of the tour he was a self-created exile. The waste of his great ability was a big loss to the side, and I couldn't help thinking again how much greater a batsman even he would have been had he a steely temperament like that of Brian Close.

Strangely my main memory of Colin on this trip is when he dropped a not-too-difficult chance offered by Ian Chappell very early on in his century of the Melbourne Test. This is not because the catch was off me, but because it could well have changed Ian's career completely, as the innings had been prefaced by a series of low scores and another one would probably have cost him his place. There goes Lady Luck again for after that Ian went from strength to strength.

Bouncers and intimidatory bowling

THE REGULARITY with which I was pulled up in Australia for intimidating the batsman would suggest I am a callous person, a bully with a hard $5\frac{1}{2}$-ounce ball in my hand and the ability to project it upwards of 80 miles per hour at a batsman some 20 yards away, not caring for life and limb.

I can honestly state that I have never bowled a delivery in my life with the intention of laying out the batsman in my sights. To unsettle, yes. As a warning of what could happen, yes. But never with the intention of putting anyone out of the game nursing a cracked skull or ribs.

I am not bouncer-happy either. I doubt very much whether I would bowl as many bouncers during a full season at home as, say, Peter Lever of Lancashire, Essex's Keith Boyce or even Surrey's Robin Jackman. Certainly not as many as Mike Procter produced in a season for Gloucestershire before his knee injury.

Again anybody counting the bouncers bowled in England in the Test series of 1972 or in 1975 would probably find my total was well below the number bowled by, say, Dennis Lillee.

No batsman likes bouncers for obvious reasons. They do present an element of danger especially on some of the county grounds in England where inadequate sightscreens make it difficult for a batsman to pick up the line and length of a ball once it has left the bowler's hand. Not all English Test grounds possess sightscreens at both ends, which makes us the odd country out of the major international sides.

At times I have lost my temper and sent down a bouncer in frustration, but generally I hope I have used the weapon sparingly. I might use it perhaps against a batsman who is becoming too brave and adventurous, trying to get on the front foot even before I have bowled. Or against one who has played a defensive role, occupying the crease without making a great effort to score. A bouncer now and again might unsettle his concentration and cause him to make a mistake.

Of course I have hit batsmen. I am not proud of it but accidents do happen. I have upset crowds when they have seen their favourite batsmen ducking and weaving when I have let the odd one go. But many have confused a bouncer with that delivery just short of a length which rises chest high.

If I was as cold-blooded as has been suggested, it would be surprising that I have been warned on so few occasions when bowling in front of the best umpires in the world, namely umpires in England, who are full-time officials standing in matches day after day.

In the main they are strict but fair and there has been no chance of pulling the wool over the eyes of such umpires as Syd Buller, Charlie Elliott – now a Test selector – Dicky Bird, Arthur Fagg and Dusty Rhodes. They would not stand for any nonsense.

And this, I believe, is the key to the whole question of intimidation and bouncers. The present law covering intimidation is sufficient if it is supported by competent umpires. We do not have much bouncer trouble in England because our umpires are competent. I'm confident it would be stamped out around the rest of the world if other umpires were on the same level. Until they are I see no reason why other countries should not borrow our umpires for the winter months.

The whole question of intimidation is an emotional one, especially when incidents occur such as New Zealand bowler Ewan Chatfield almost dying on the field, or when Indian batsmen come under the hammer from West Indian fast bowlers as they did in the Caribbean in 1976. And when emotions are involved, the picture is often distorted. The question is so complex that I do not think it can be helped by bringing in more rules and limitations, because there are so many factors to be taken into consideration already, including the ability of the man at the wicket and the condition of the wicket.

The answer must lie with the umpires, the men closest to the spot. If they are good enough there will be no trouble. If they are not, they should be replaced. Really, it is as simple as that.

Looking back I can only remember four warnings with any detail during my bowling life in England and two of those were in the same season in the summer of 1967, when I was trying to break into the England side as the regular opening bowler. Both of them came on wickets which helped expose the batsmen to danger.

The first was at Edgbaston where Sussex batted first and were rolled over for 104, Warwickshire left-arm spinner Jim Allan returning career-best figures of five for 11. Then it was the turn of Tony Buss and myself on the unpredictable wicket on which two balls pitched within half an inch of each other produced entirely different results.

Half the Warwickshire side had been shot out for 46 and the unfortunate John Jameson was on his way to hospital, where an X-ray confirmed a broken bone in his left hand, by the time umpire George Pope warned me for bowling too many bouncers.

John's injury had been the result of the second delivery he faced from me in my fifth over. It reared up and caught him as he tried to fend it away. Off he went and my next ball also reared up catching the edge of Alan Smith's bat. Other deliveries had reacted the same way earlier in my spell.

George Pope stepped in when Billy Ibadulla received a couple of deliveries around his head in my next over. They were not particularly short, but the extraordinary bounce coupled with Billy's rather small frame made them look vicious enough. George held up the game while he spoke to Bill Copson, who was standing at square leg, before walking back to me, wagging his finger. I realised, too, that the wicket was dangerous after the Ibadulla incidents, and made sure I pitched the ball further up for the remainder of the innings, even though it made life a little easier for the batsmen.

Despite having half the Warwickshire side out for 46 we still had to surrender first innings lead and points that went with the lead in those days. John Jameson returned from hospital to find Warwickshire on 97 for nine and bravely volunteered to go in again. He had his left hand strapped up but decided to bat the "wrong way round" so that he could steer the bat with his right hand and stayed in with last man Jack Bannister to take Warwickshire ahead. The match was drawn in the end.

My second blitz that season came against Gloucestershire at Bristol. Actually I was not warned by the umpires on this occasion although the Bristol crowd became pretty hostile and demanded that I should be taken off.

Again it all happened late in the day after we had been bowled out for 172 on another unpredictable wicket. By the end of that first day Gloucestershire were 108 for five, four of the wickets going to me. The trouble arose because I hit three of the batsmen before taking their wickets.

Ron Nicholls was the first when I cut a ball back which lifted a little as well to catch him on the top of the thigh. Soon afterwards he spooned a simple catch from a stroke ringsiders described as a "protective jab."

My next ball cracked new batsman Sid Russell on the forearm sending him off to hospital and later I hit David Shepherd on the foot which had him hobbling painfully for the rest of his short innings. I "bagged' him in the end, and also Russell when he came back after a hospital examination had shown his arm was not broken.

My hitting John Jameson and the three Gloucestershire players was unfortunate. I did not mean to do it but it is very difficult to know exactly where to bowl on wickets where no two balls react the same way. Pitch one shortish and it becomes a long hop and easy meat for the batsman. Pitch another just half an inch away and it rises up in an alarming manner. We have far too many wickets like that in this country.

My other warning that summer came at Canterbury late in the season in the Kent second innings which they started 112 runs ahead and looking well placed for victory.

It was a fast track, one of the fastest I had encountered that season and in complete contrast to the Headingley wicket from which I had just come after playing for England against Pakistan.

Mike Denness got the worst of it immediately after lunch on that second day when he cracked me for a couple of fours driven off the front foot. It was time for a warning that things were not that easy. I gave him a couple of bouncers in an over which brought umpire Ron Lay into action. He warned me and Jim Parks, the Sussex captain, and spoke to the other umpire Cec Pepper.

I still let Mike have another in my next over and it brought his wicket when he failed to get his gloves out of the way and gave a catch behind to Jim Parks. I admit I was annoyed at the time. After the way that Mike had struck me for a couple of fours I thought that Ron Lay was a little hasty in stepping in when I tried to use a legitimate weapon for a fast bowler.

Despite getting Mike's wicket I was still upset when Stuart Leary came in to take his place and I let him have a couple of bouncers too. Stuart showed his annoyance by walking down the wicket and tapping down an imaginary hole nearer my end than his. Ron Lay showed *his* annoyance by again warning Jim Parks and myself. He also spoke to Cec Pepper. It was my last warning and I had no alternative but to bowl at a much fuller length during the rest of the innings.

The final warning I can recall came in 1970 in a match against Glamorgan at Hove.

Again it was a wicket producing quite a bit of unpredictable bounce. The trouble started towards the end of the Glamorgan first innings when their last man Laurence Williams was forced to duck under one delivery I pitched a little short.

Later in the same over I was a bit short again. This time Williams lost sight of the ball and was struck on the back when he turned away. Nothing was said to me at the time by the umpires Dusty Rhodes and Lloyd Budd although one spectator took exception and hurled abuse at me during the rest of the over.

The warning came in Glamorgan's second innings as they were stumbling to defeat despite some poor fielding on our part which saw five chances spilled in the slips.

The one danger man was Len Hill, a solid and stubborn batsman who was a little short on strokes but made up for it with unlimited patience and sound concentration. We could not afford to have him around for too long and I decided to give him a bouncer or two in an effort to unsettle him before he became adjusted to the conditions.

On my count I gave him two bouncers in one over. Dusty Rhodes totted up and made it three which he considered was one bouncer too many and warned me for intimidatory bowling. Mike Griffith, Sussex captain, agreed with my count when Dusty called him over and he had to accept a finger-wigging lecture in the middle of the wicket for arguing.

Try as I might I cannot recall any other instances when I have fallen foul of the umpires strictly on the question of intimidatory bowling.

I have have had a few ups and downs with them on other matters, of course, mainly on the question of running on the wicket. That has been my biggest problem and it happens on two grounds in particular.

I have been warned more times for running on the wicket in my follow through at Canterbury and Lord's than on any other grounds. It is more than pure coincidence.

Both grounds slope, which means that the ground is falling away from under my feet when I bowl from the pavilion end at Lord's and towards the pavilion at Canterbury – the two ends fast bowlers favour on these grounds. The fall is slight. But it is just enough to make me drift into the danger area and the only counter is to bowl from a little wider of the stumps than I want to.

The point of illustrating these "bouncer" incidents is to show that they have largely been due to wickets of variable bounce, but even then if the bowler is controlled promptly and fairly intimidation can be checked. It is when neither batsman and bowler know how the ball will behave after it pitches that most accidents occur. Any criticism of unreliable wickets would have to include those at Lord's and Sydney, in my experience, and these are supposed to be top grounds.

Aside from wickets of variable bounce, most injuries are caused by batsman mis-hooking, which is not the fault of the bowlers. Two incidents of this come from each end of my career. A long time ago Greg Chappell, then of Somerset, hooked me into his face and needed stitches, while in Perth in 1976 Alvin Kallicharan did the same thing against Dennis Lillee, and broke his nose. Such injuries as these have occurred regularly since the bouncer was invented.

1971: Dropped by Sussex for not trying

BACK FROM Australia, my cricketing troubles all came to a head in 1971. I was criticised for my manner and approach when playing for England in Australia; banned by England at home from playing in a Test match against India; and hauled before the Sussex committee at Hove to answer a charge that I had not been trying in a county championship match – probably the most damaging indictment that can be made against a professional player.

I was not only charged but found guilty, reprimanded, and dropped from the Sussex team as a punishment because it was felt my attitude and approach might jeopardise the morale of the rest of the side if it went unchecked. Now was the summer of my discontent.

As a result of my four months in Australia reclaiming the Ashes and living my boyhood dream, I looked at cricket in a different light that summer when I picked up the threads of the domestic scene. Much of what I saw made me indignant.

Perhaps the most annoying part of the Sussex statement after my "trial" was the claim that my attitude might jeopardise the morale of the rest of the side if it went unchecked. That was a laugh for anybody who knew the dressing room feeling at the time.

The mood had changed in the first summer of Mike Griffith's captaincy but the sense of hopelessness and frustration had gradually crept back when the senior players realised he would be no more successful in beating the system than previous captains and began to question his qualifications as a leader.

Most of the links with the past had been broken with Ken Suttle's career ending at the finish of the 1970 season. Roger Prideaux switched from Northamptonshire to take his place but the middle order batting lacked the experience so desperately needed.

Ken's departure left the dressing room dominated by players who had never known success with the county, and the prospect of tasting any were receding year by year as the committee appeared content to sit back unconcerned, growing more distant all the time.

The players were still keen and ambitious. As professionals they kept going because of their professional pride in their own performance, but there was little encouragement from the club itself to weld the group of individuals into a team with a purpose and a future. We could all see that the lack of ambition and drive at the top was pulling the county down.

There was a front of politeness between the players and the members of the committee but we were worlds apart with seemingly no way of bridging that gap although we attempted to stretch a hand across.

During that summer a group of the more senior players tried to make their views known to the committee and we thought we had got somewhere when told to put our complaints, points of view and future plans to the then secretary Arthur Dumbrell – along the proper lines of communication.

For an hour or more we sat talking with Mr Dumbrell in the dressing room explaining our fears and our hopes. At last we felt things were moving as Mr Dumbrell sat, listened, made notes and points of his own.

The arguments covered many aspects but lo and behold all our efforts came to nothing at the end of the meeting when we asked Mr Dumbrell if he would raise them before the full committee, and he said: "No." On the grounds that *he* thought we had not made any valid points. What could we do, for Mr Dumbrell, according to the committee, was the proper line of communication between playing staff and employers. When we tried to use it we found it was cut.

After that I tried to talk to club chairman Doug Wilshin and Eddie Harrison, chairman of the cricket committee, to explain the situation but it was to have very little effect – if any. I even went as far as telling them bluntly the mood at the club would not change so long as we did not have a decent captain and while the management stayed as it was. But they offered Mike Griffith the captaincy for a further two-year period at the end of the season. I thought Mike was wrong to accept, knowing how the players felt.

I could never imagine Mike being forceful enough in his dealings with the committee to break down the "them and us" attitude which ran through the club. Us being the players, the servants of the club. Them being the privileged few who drank gin and tonic, gave the orders, and expected them to be carried out without question or argument. The running of the club in those days had just not kept pace with the growth of professionalism on the field and did not show any sign of ever catching up.

That attitude still exists in some quarters although it is a lot easier now that Tony Greig has taken charge. In one of his first statements on becoming captain he said he wished to get rid of the "gin and tonic" image of Sussex. It caused quite an uproar at the time but he has partially succeeded in his attempt. Tony Greig and

Mike Griffith are two entirely different characters. Tony is the big, blond extrovert type, Mike fairly shy and retiring. I do not think Mike particularly liked or enjoyed his years as captain and I had the impression that perhaps he accepted the role because it was expected of him.

Although I have critcised him as a leader I have to qualify it by saying that he took over in a difficult period. Ian Thomson had already gone, Alan Oakman retired at the end of the 1968 season, Ken Suttle was nearing the end, Ted Dexter was only an occasional player and there was no "Tiger" Pataudi. The committee had failed to provide him with suitable replacements, or a balanced side.

His spirit had to be admired too. A very good fielder, nippy when running between the wickets, he was also a gutsy batsman even if he did not quite make the runs in his first-class career that he promised to at one stage. He would chip in with his thirties, forties and fifties, more often than not when the wicket was a little difficult and the side was struggling for runs having lost the main batsmen early.

Our differences really came into the open early in the summer of 1971 after I had returned from Australia. They resulted in me being dropped from the side. The consequences reached beyond the Sussex borders for that dropping meant that I was overlooked by England for the three-match series against Pakistan in the first half of the summer.

In addition to recovering from the injury to my right hand I was whacked when I arrived back in England from the MCC tour. Played out mentally and physically, my back troubled me from the strain of bowling on the harder Australian wickets for four months and my right shoulder had "gone" when it came to throwing the ball in. I was still not fit when the English season started and missed the odd game because of my aches and strains. I was nowhere near my best.

My shoulder was the catalyst of my troubles with Sussex. I could still bowl although I was not doing well at the time. But I could not throw. That may sound strange but it is common enough complaint with cricketers. The two require completely different actions.

I made Mike Griffith quite aware of my difficulties yet he still insisted on putting me down on the fine leg boundary in the match against Warwickshire at Hove where all the trouble started. That annoyed me for a start because it just did not make tactical sense. My temper became worse the longer the Warwickshire innings lasted and the more exposed I became.

It did not take John Jameson long to discover that I could not get the ball back to the wicket quickly and he was soon working the ball off his legs down towards my direction at the boundary looking for an easy two runs.

For all his bulk – and that is mainly around the chest region – Jameson is still fairly spritely over 22 yards and he was nipping in for a second run even when I had the ball in my hands. And beating the ball back with yards to spare.

What made it seem worse was my apparent lack of effort in the field. I knew there was no point in dashing round the boundary to cut off a possible second run when they were going to take a second anyway because I could not get the ball back fast enough.

Instead of the dash one would expect I loped round to pick up the ball. That upset the members as well as Griffith. Yet none of this would have happened if Griffith had placed me nearer the bat.

Be that as it may, it made little difference when I was hauled up yet again before the Sussex committee and condemned to a spell in the wilderness. I was also instructed to write to Eddie Harrison and Mike Griffith apologising for my manners towards them. It happened as the count down was beginning for the first Test against Pakistan and obviously put me out of the running, although I doubt whether I would have been fit anyway.

The statement secretary Arthur Dumbrell issued to the newspapers was short and to the point. It read:

> 'The selection committee have decided to drop John Snow as a result of his recent performances in Championship matches.
>
> 'His bowling performances, and more especially his fielding have been so lacking in effort that the selection committee had no alternative.
>
> 'While recognising the great physical strain of bowling fast they felt that John Snow's indifferent attitude, if left unchecked, would jeopardise the morale of the rest of the side.'

There was no answer to that, at least none that I was allowed to give in the lop-sided arrangements contracts produce, although I would have liked to have challenged that statement for the reasons I have already given. I could not because of a clause in every cricketer's contract which denies him the right of free speech and prevents him giving his views to the media. A clause that would never stand up, I am sure, if challenged in a court.

It means that a county club can say anything it likes about the conduct or behaviour of its players subject to the laws of slander and libel. A player however may not give his version of any incidents because he is supposed to have every public utterance cleared by his own county club before it appears in print, on radio or television. There was nothing I could do or say to defend myself without risking being banned.

As it turned out the sacking from the first team was a blessing in disguise. I had tried to play for Sussex when I was not fit because it was expected of me after helping to recover the Ashes in Australia just three months before. I did not, in fact, play for the second eleven as the Sussex committee hoped. Instead I placed myself in the care of my doctor who confirmed I wasn't fit to play cricket and ordered me to rest completely to allow my back and shoulder to mend.

Naturally the sacking made headline news the next day and the cricket writers were split into two camps – predictably enough. The so-called "quality" papers took the county line with reference to my past misdemeanours on the field; the "popular" papers offered sympathy, recognising the demands made on me by England and the difficulty of trying to serve both masters at once.

It is difficult at home. Whenever a Test match has come into sight and I have been selected I have always tried to save something during the Sussex championship match immediately prior to the Test, the situation permitting. It is essential that if possible I build a reserve to draw upon for the extra effort required in a Test when bowling against four or five top-line batsmen instead of the one or two in an opposing county line-up. Consequently my performances for Sussex have not always been sparkling throughout those games.

Sussex have sometimes suffered also on my return from Test matches especially if I have been required to do a lot of work. That has often left me spent physically on my return to county duty. When playing on tour it's often possible to miss the game before a Test which makes it easier. Even the one after it sometimes. So although bowling in the Test is harder work on tour, the overall job is easier.

Test matches also require great mental effort, and there is a psychological let-down after them. I find it very hard to raise my game and enthusiasm returning to play before a couple of hundred people after five days appearing before 20,000 on a Test ground. With double tours these days resulting in Test matches every other weekend at the height of the season, there is little time for the building-up process and the readjustment afterwards.

It has meant a great reduction in the number of championship matches when I have felt able to give my all for Sussex and my wicket-taking rate has suffered. I cannot argue with that. Except to say I do not think I am an exception. I can remember hearing grumbles from Surrey members about Geoff Arnold's championship return in 1973 when he finished with only 30 or so wickets. The poor chap had bowled his heart out for England that summer in three matches against New Zealand and another three against the West Indies.

It was because of Test calls interrupting my duties for Sussex that I turned down the suggestion that I should take over the county captaincy early in the 1970s. Yes, that's right. The chance of being Sussex captain.

The suggestion was made during one of my discussions with Doug Wilshin, chairman of the Sussex committee, when I was complaining about the lack of success and ambition at the club. Whether the idea would have got beyond Mr Wilshin and been acceptable to the other committee members, I doubt, but I never gave it a chance of going any further. I refused to let the possibility take root because I felt that the county, in the position they found themselves at the time, needed a full-time captain whose attention would not be diverted by Test appearances.

After I had been dropped it was almost a month before I played cricket again. The series against Pakistan was all but finished and the first Test against India at Lord's was only a fortnight away. At the time of my censure by the club I had taken only three wickets for 223 runs but I confirmed that all was well again on my return by taking 11 wickets for 108 in a match against Essex, helping Sussex to their second win of the season.

Those wickets could not have come at a better time – just before the selectors were meeting to select the team for the first Test against India. Perhaps, as things turned out, it might have been better if I had taken none for plenty against Essex instead.

1971: Gavaskar. England drop me – again

NONE OF the incidents in which I have been involved either at home or overseas caused as much furore as that day at Lord's in the summer of 1971 when India's little opening batsman Sunil Gavaskar bit the dust and I was banned from England's next Test match as punishment.

I shall never forget that clash of bodies, or all the fuss it caused. No doubt many millions who watched it countless times on television will never forget the slow motion version.

I was wrong. I realised that as soon as my shoulder came into contact with Gavaskar. In that instant I could imagine the horror on the faces of everybody watching the game from the committee room at Lord's, and on a few more faces besides.

But I do not think the incident would have provoked all the arguments and fuss it did if it had not been for the presence of the television cameras and their slow motion replays. The actual bodily contact between us was over in a flash. On the slow motion replays it took a minute or two to go through the whole scene and allow the full impact to register.

For a long time professional footballers have been complaining of trial by television with the slow motion replays showing foul tackles in close up and in great detail. The footballers have not tried to excuse their offences against the laws of the game by the fact that they often look worse than they actually are when seen out of context.

I, too, do not excuse my action at Lord's that summer during the Indian second innings. Except to say that I had no intention of knocking Gavaskar over. I was quite prepared to accept what punishment was coming my way and fully accept that the authorities – whoever they were – had no alternative but to be seen to act after what had been shown on television that morning and again during the evening in the news bulletins.

What did upset me were the scenes of near-hysteria which took place in the England dressing room at the lunch interval a few minutes after the incident, when heated demands were made that I should apologise to Gavaskar immediately. The actual incident was only part of the trouble. What, apparently, had inflamed many officials is the fact that I tossed the bat to Gavaskar afterwards instead of handing it to him in a so-called gentlemanly way. More of that later.

Let me take you through the scene as I saw it during that over just before lunch on the final day of the match, with India making their bid for victory. They had taken a first innings lead of nine runs when scoring 313 and had bowled us out for 191 in our second innings which left them needing 183 for victory.

We had made a quick break-through when Mankad was caught behind off my bowling and captain Wadekar mishooked a ball from John Price to Geoff Boycott at short mid-wicket. India were then 21 for two and in serious trouble. Farohk Engineer was promoted to join Gavaskar and immediately started to launch a counter-attack.

The partnership had more than doubled the score and lunch was approaching when I began that troublesome over. Engineer was facing me and he turned one delivery on the leg side, not really hitting it by just rolling the ball in the direction of mid-wicket and mid-on, only a yard or so off the actual wicket. He called for a sharp single.

There was no fielder near enough to threaten the single. Only me falling away to the other side of the wicket as I continued on my follow through. Engineer himself was safe. The only man in possible danger was Gavaskar if I could get to the ball and take a pot shot at the wicket at the batsman's end.

My follow-through had taken me ahead of Gavaskar, of course, but with the ball being on the opposite side of the wicket to me I suppose we were about equal distance from it when I started to change direction and Gavaskar began to respond urgently to Engineer's shout. As I went for the ball the first thing that went through my mind was that Gavaskar would do the one thing all batsmen are taught and expected to do when they find themselves in that type of situation. Namely to run over the ball – which was in his path – and so baulk the attempt by the fielder to pick it up.

It was going to be a close race as to who reached the ball first. Or so I thought. I expected some measure of bodily contact and steeled myself for it as I neared the ball. In fact I did more than that. I made sure I would get it and that proved my undoing.

That physical challenge from Gavaskar – yes, all 5ft 4in of him – never came. Instead of trying to run over the ball he ran wider of the wicket to avoid me. By "pushing" over to my right I went that way as well. Unbalanced, I was in no position to pick up the ball and merely crashed into Gavaskar instead. In the end all the weight of the bodily contact came from me.

As I said earlier, the moment I made contact and Gavaskar started to fall I could sense the shocked silence in the MCC committee room.

I knew I was going to be in trouble. For a moment I did not know what to do while Sunny Gavaskar picked himself up. Then I saw his bat in front of me and, after he had brushed himself down, I picked it up and gently tossed it to him. We were no more than a yard apart. I could quite easily have taken a step and handed it to him but it seemed such a natural act to spin it to him the way kids spin a bat to decide who is going to bat or bowl.

I cannot honestly recall whether any words passed between us at that moment. I don't mean angry words. I was certainly not angry with him nor he with me. He looked a little startled, perhaps – and no wonder. The only words I can remember were those of umpire David Constant who came down the wicket and said to me: "Come on now, we can't have any of that."

I finished the over which took us up to lunch but, by that time, I expect I had already been found guilty of ungentlemanly conduct by everybody who watched the slow motion replays on television. Certainly I had been judged by those people who were watching it in the committee room at Lord's.

As I walked into the England dressing room at lunch time Alec Bedser was coming in from the players' balcony where he had been watching the last session of the morning's play. I immediately apologised to him.

"Sorry about that, Big Al," I remember saying to him. "It was a bit unfortunate, wasn't it."

"You'll apologise, won't you?" he said.

"Sure," I replied. "Just let me get my shirt off and wipe away the sweat."

With that I sat down to put on another shirt ready to go along to the Indian dressing room when the door burst open and in stormed Billy Griffith, secretary of MCC. I don't think I've ever seen a man look so angry. He was literally white with rage as he shouted at me: "That's the most disgusting thing I've ever seen on the field."

I told him I'd already had a word with Alec Bedser about the incident but Mr Griffith kept on at me. An argument erupted until Ray Illingworth intervened and suggested to Mr Griffith it would be better if he left the dressing room. He did this, followed by Ray, who "had a go" at him for coming into the dressing room in the first place.

The whole of this incident was brought up again equally noisily before the match against the West Indies at the Oval in 1973. It was at the pre-Test dinner and all the selectors were there, and it could well have affected my further selection, hardening one or two opinions that I was a thorn in the flesh. I was dropped after that game.

I'm afraid I was in no mood to have apologised after that outburst.

I needed the lunch break to calm down. If I had walked down the corridor filled with Members to reach the Indian dressing room I do not think a gracious apology would have followed. Particularly if on the way any other Members had made a comment. I thought it better to wait.

My apology to Gavaskar came immediately after the luncheon interval when he was at the Nursery End and I walked past him to get to my fielding position.

"Sorry about that," I said. "It was very unfortunate. Are you okay?"

"Yes," he replied. "It was just one of those things."

That was all that passed between us at that moment. No lengthy show, no obvious chat that the crowd or the television cameras picked up. But the act had been carried out and Gavaskar was perfectly happy and content about it.

Later that evening I had time to apologise more fully when we had a drink or two together. There was no animosity, no ill feeling between us. He accepted the apology and repeated that it was just one of those things. India's manager Hemu Adhikari also accepted the situation and announced that the matter was closed so far as he was concerned.

It wasn't so far as the others were concerned, of course. The debate and furore was to go on for several days with some people demanding that I should be dropped from the next Test side as a lesson, some arguing that I should never be allowed to play for England again and still others calling for an official reprimand to warn me as to future conduct but without interfering with my Test career.

I knew the last would not happen. I knew too that being dropped from the next Test match was the minimum sentence I would receive, although there would be no court and I would not be given any chance to speak up for myself.

I could understand the authorities would want to take some action to help protect the image of the game after the television exposure, so I was quite prepared for the call on the following Saturday when I was summoned to speak to Alec Bedser on the telephone. The England side for the second Test at Old Trafford was being announced that morning. I was playing for Sussex against Hampshire at Portsmouth.

What I wasn't prepared for was the explanation of Alec Bedser. He told me I was being left out of the next Test match. Then he added that this wasn't a decision of the England selectors, but a direct order from above.

That rankled with me. Somebody else was issuing orders to the selectors before they had a chance to take any action themselves.

I told Alec: "If you are sending messages one way you can send a message back. Tell them they can stuff themselves."

Wrong, of course. But I was in no mood for niceties at that particular moment. Throughout my playing career I've never really known where I stood or who was pulling the strings. I always felt there was somebody else in the background doing some manipulating, and this confirmed my suspicions.

It wasn't announced that way, of course. Alec Bedser issued a press statement in which he said:

> 'Snow was not considered for this match for disciplinary reasons. My committee and I intend to ensure to the best of our ability that the game of cricket is conducted at all times in the right manner.'

I agree with those sentiments. It was a sad way to end the match for me after my batting in the first innings for England when I had visions – briefly – of scoring a century for England at Lord's. We had been in a fair bit of trouble when I went in and I finished top scorer with 73 runs, a googly from Chandrasekhar finally proving my undoing.

Several times since that match I have wondered what would have happened if the incident had involved Farokh Engineer instead of Gavaskar. Farokh was about my own height and a stone heavier.

Nothing had been said, for instance, about a similar incident three years earlier in the West Indies during the last Test in Georgetown, Guyana.

Again I was bowling. Again there was a chance of a run out if I could get to the ball quickly and have a throw at the wickets. Again there was a tangle of bodies in a physical confrontation. Only this time the body happened to belong to Clive Lloyd who towers some five inches above me and has a weight advantage of at least a couple of stone. Clive bit the dust that day. So did I. With Clive on top of me, trampling on me as he tried to regain his feet and the crease. Nobody said a word on that occasion.

The incident was further inflamed by Sussex where, upon hearing that I had been dropped from the England side, Sussex secretary Arthur Dumbrell released a statement saying that Sussex might consider taking disciplinary action against me. A statement I later understood he had no right to make, as it had not been before the committee. At Portsmouth I tackled club chairman Eddie Harrison about Dumbrell's statement and he told me he knew nothing about it. That caused an outburst from me for it confirmed that the running of Sussex cricket was in a mess, and increased my frustration.

Sunny Gavaskar and I were to meet up again later that summer, a completely unexpected meeting so far as I was concerned.

The Lord's Test match was drawn, rain sweeping over the ground at tea on the last day with England needing another two wickets and India wanting another 38 runs. Although Solkar was at the wicket, the odds must have favoured England with Bedi his partner and just Chandra to come.

The next Test at Old Trafford also finished in a draw with the weather definitely saving India. Peter Lever had replaced me in the England team as partner to John Price and together they had done a good job, enough to retain their places when the side was selected for the final match at the Oval. My ban was for one Test match only but I couldn't complain about being overlooked.

I got my entry ticket back into the England team when John Price reported to the Oval and said he was doubtful. Sussex were not playing and I received a call on the Wednesday afternoon asking me to report to the Oval. It came out of the blue and I was unable to get to the ground until Thursday morning, to find that I was back in the side and starting at 11.30. To me it just wasn't a Test match. I thought I was there as a last resort and in any case was pretty cynical after the Lord's episode and its surrounding clamour. Mentally unprepared, I felt like I would before a club match.

My meeting with Sunny Gavaskar was remarkable for he almost ended up on his backside again. Only this time nobody could have complained.

It happened when a shortish delivery lifted and went through about chin high – remember he is only 5ft 4in tall. He got himself in a tangle trying to avoid it and in the end the ball missed the underside of his chin by a fraction of an inch. Close enough to part the chain and medallion he was wearing around his neck.

We lost that Test match. It was the first time Ray Illingworth had been beaten by another country since he had taken over the captaincy of England from Colin Cowdrey in the summer of 1969, his only other defeats being at the hands of the Rest of the World side in 1970. It was the first time I had been on the losing England side since the summer of 1968 – a run of 22 matches.

There was another first as a result of that game. It was the first time that India – winners on a tour of the Caribbean before coming to England – had won a Test match on English soil. Yet, coming late into the match as I did, I could not feel too depressed about the outcome, although I dislike losing.

The result apart, my England career had finished on a happier note than at the beginning of the summer, but the Sussex scene was starting to deteriorate rapidly. With Ted Dexter returning for a season of Sunday matches and giving us the benefit of his tactical flair in the "instant" form of cricket, we at last climbed off the bottom of the John Player League and just managed to finish in the top half of the table.

The championship, however, was a different story as we dropped two places for the second successive season, and the Gillette Cup saw us knocked out at the first attempt. The fears I had expressed to the Sussex committee were beginning to become realities. But still nothing appeared to be done to arrest the slide.

1972: Tony Greig. Australians in England

THE EVIDENCE of Sussex's decline was there for all to see in 1972. After the initial surge following the appointment of Mike Griffith as captain, we were back where we were in 1968. The dressing room atmosphere was unhappy and disenchanted, with the inevitable consequences: we finished last but one in the championship, only two places off the bottom in the John Player League, and were knocked out of the Gillette Cup before the competition became interesting.

The message was clear enough, and Mike announced he was giving up the captaincy at the end of the summer. Again I was well away from the scene when the announcement was made, just as I had been when Jim Parks relinquished the job four seasons before. I was up at Old Trafford playing for England in the one-day Prudential Cup series against Australia.

Immediately I heard the news my thoughts went, once more, to Tony Buss as the best person to take over the task, but it was Tony Greig who received a phone call in Manchester which sent him dashing down to Hove.

Tony Buss was still my choice at that time for the same reasons I put forward when I thought he should have taken over from Jim Parks. His experience, tactical sense and age were ideal, and he would be with Sussex the whole time. I felt the last was essential.

I had no doubts that Tony Greig would be captain one day but I thought that day was probably another two years off, after Tony Buss had laid down the necessary foundations of the rebuilding work. My doubts about Greigy concerned his age, for he was then 25, his lack of tactical experience and the fact that he was only just settling into the England side. I thought it was asking too much of him to try to revitalise an ailing side and at the same time to concentrate on securing a regular place at Test level.

As it has turned out Greigy has proved a winner. He has been able to combine his two roles, although it has put a tremendous weight on his shoulders, a weight increased when he was appointed England captain in 1975 to succeed Mike Denness. I hope all the responsibility doesn't take its toll too early.

His keenness, enthusiasm and will-to-win stirred up the whole team and have continued to do so, even if the final placings in the championship have not been all that impressive under his reign so far. The same thing happened when he took over with England. At both county and country level Tony has led from the front, and the "troops" have not been slow to follow.

He had one distinct advantage when it came to Sussex affairs in that he was an "outsider," having come over from South Africa. He could see and sense what was wrong with the organisation and what needed to be done, not having been blinded by familiarity as many were who grew up with the club and knew no other influence.

During his early years he listened, too, when the senior players discussed the problems and I knew he agreed with our sentiments, so that when he did take over he was aware of what was required. I believe his two or three seasons under Ray Illingworth in the England side were very important, for he came into the England dressing room when the senior players were of a reforming nature. He is strong enough to say what he thinks and his appointment as England captain has also strengthened his arm when it comes to making demands of the Sussex committee.

There are still occasions however, when I question his tactical direction, for I often feel his ideas are rather too ambitious, particularly in the field. He tends to be a very excitable captain, and in his determination to prove who is master shows the impetuous streak he often displays in his batting.

At times this impetuous streak has proved costly in giving away runs yet it has also brought results when least expected. Perhaps the most important factor in his captaincy with Sussex is his willingness to listen to others and act on their suggestions. The result has been the players all feel part of a team and know exactly what is expected of them and what they are trying to do.

With the way things were going in Sussex during Mike Griffith's last year it was a relief to have my mind fully occupied for half the season attempting to keep the Ashes against Australia, a summer when Dennis Lillee first made an impact on the crowds in this country and showed what a fine bowler he is.

The summer of 1972 was Lillee's despite that freakish Test match at Lord's when Bob Massie took advantage of the conditions to finish the game with 16 wickets and enter his name in the record books. His bowling performance pulled Ian Chappell's Australian side back into the series after we had beaten them in the opening game at Old Trafford.

It was also the summer during which Greg Chappell emerged as a complete all-round batsman, growing from the rather limited player

I knew when he first played in England for Somerset and developing further after that century he had taken off us when making his Test debut in Perth during the 1970–71 tour.

We were to see all three of them – Massie, Lillee and Greg Chappell – at their best in that strange Lord's Test match, for although Massie took the wickets he would be the first to admit that he owed many of them to the fire and control of Lillee rushing in from the other end. Lillee was very difficult to score against. We tried to take them off Massie instead and paid the penalty as he produced a rich mixture of well-disguised inswingers and outswingers during those rather startling days.

It was remarkable how everything went for the Australians during that match and I am not taking anything away from their victory. You still have to have the bowlers and the batsmen to take advantage of the conditions when they are in your favour. The atmospheric conditions helped Massie and encouraged swing bowling when we batted first, and the medium-paced bowler from Western Australia captured eight wickets.

The conditions had improved when it came to the Australian's turn to reply. They were still not easy but the sun had strengthened and there was not so much help for us. It was in that innings that Greg Chappell first impressed me with his all-round ability when rescuing his side.

He went through a very sticky period when he first came in, brother Ian doing most of the scoring when they were at the wicket together, yet he never allowed his narrow escapes to affect his concentration or his determination. He was at the wicket almost three hours before he scored his first boundary, but when Ian was out and left him the stage he firmly took control.

I can once remember getting Greg into all sorts of trouble when I bowled a bouncer at him during a Sussex match against Somerset. He attempted to hook me over mid-wicket but top-edged the ball into his face. It was a painful blow but he still retained his sense of humour, saying: "I don't want anybody to tell me ever again that I can hook."

Although the promise was there even then he was a very limited player, and those limitations were still there when he scored that century against us in Perth. It was a fine innings but he was forced to concentrate on the leg side for most of his runs. However, by the time of the 1972 Test at Lord's, he was playing his strokes freely all round the wicket. During his innings of 131, we saw him maturing before our very eyes.

It was towards the end of Australia's innings that the atmospheric conditions started to change again, making a hazy, muggy day. I can remember bowling to Dennis Lillee after lunch on the Saturday and noticing the difference immediately. I thought to myself then that luck was with them. I could almost see the wicket "greening up" before my eyes and here we were bowling them out so that they could take advantage of it. They did that in no uncertain terms.

We were all fascinated watching Massie in action from the England dressing room balcony and wondered what else he had in store for us during the rest of the series. He was so devastating at Lord's. We were not really put at rest by John Edrich when he remarked: "Ian Chappell's overbowled him in this match. I don't think he'll be the same again on the tour."

How right John proved to be. But Massie still had the most remarkable delivery of that summer up his sleeve, and John Edrich was his victim.

It came in the drawn third Test match at Trent Bridge, on a wicket that grew better as the days went by. It really was a beauty. He bowled round the wicket to John and by the time the ball reached the return crease it looked as if it could end up going for a wide. That's when it started to bend, swinging in an astonishing amount to bowl John, who was completely mesmerised. None of us had never seen a ball like it. Apart from that ball, Massie was generally ineffective after Lord's, partly due to our batting outside the crease, forcing him to bowl shorter and giving the ball less time to swing.

For excitement and drama even the Lord's match was overshadowed by the fourth game at Headingley, a match which had the Australians screaming that the wicket had been fixed to suit Derek Underwood as we won inside three days to go ahead in the series once more.

Norman Gifford had started that summer as the first choice slow left-arm bowler in the England side, playing in the first three Tests on wickets that did not give him any real encouragement. He had taken quite a hammering when Rodney Marsh unleashed a fierce and desperate onslaught in the first Test at Old Trafford and the critics were demanding Derek Underwood's recall as each Test went by. The fourth Test at Headingley saw the change and heightened the Australian suspicions of foul play for Derek hustled them to an innings defeat.

It was a wicket that suited Derek's pace and style down to the ground. It had been attacked by a fungi called fusarium and been flooded three or four days before the match by a heavy thunderstorm. The Australians were unwilling to believe that simple explanation.

When we looked at it on the Wednesday afternoon before the Test match we all thought the game would be over in four days.

The wicket looked as though it would not last and we all felt that the side winning the toss and batting first would take the match. We were not all that hopeful, therefore, when Ian Chappell won the toss and our fears grew when Australia made a steady start, losing only one wicket before lunch, that of Ross Edwards who opened with Keith Stackpole.

Then Derek got to work by dismissing Stackpole, and from that moment the Australians went to pieces, being bowled out for 146. Even that looked a healthy total when we struggled in turn. We were seven down for 128 when I went out to join Ray Illingworth. I played an innings that day which must rank as one of my most valuable in Test cricket, making 48 before I was stumped against the occasional left-arm spin bowling of John Inverarity. It helped win the game.

Ray was superb at the other end as we put on 104 for the eighth wicket. He knew that the Australian collapse in the first innings had given us a chance of taking the match but he still feared batting last. We needed a good first innings lead and he made sure that we got one. It was enough to win the game.

When the Australians started their second innings Geoff Arnold whipped in for a couple of early wickets and once Derek Underwood started to turn his arm over that was the end. The Australian dressing room was an unhappy place that night as they grew more and more suspicious of the combination of the wicket and Derek Underwood's timely recall to the England side.

In fact they should have won the game having had the best of the conditions when batting first, but try telling that to an Australian and he looks at you in disbelief. I was in Australia the following winter playing for the Carlton Club in Melbourne and everywhere I went the subject of Headingley came up. The Australians just would not accept that they were beaten fairly and squarely, although I suspect Keith Stackpole recognised the truth. At the end of the match he was very bitter about the Australian batting performance in both innings.

That victory put us 2–1 ahead with the final Test at the Oval to come, a match remarkable for the performance of the Chappell brothers, who each scored a century in the Australian first innings, the only instance of brothers scoring hundreds in the same Test innings. They swung the game Australia's way.

The match was also a painful one for Ray Illingworth and myself. He twisted his ankle on the penultimate day which put him out of the rest of the match and I suffered a bruised left wrist, of all things, which meant I couldn't bowl on the last day as the Australians chased the 242 runs they needed to win.

The wrist had been on the receiving end of a Dennis Lillee bouncer towards the end of the England second innings and by the last morning – when Australia needed another 128 to win with eight wickets left – it was throbbing painfullly. I tried to bowl but it was useless. My rhythm was destroyed and my direction suffered all because of that bruised wrist on my non-bowling hand. Many people could not understand why I did not bowl more especially as Basil D'Oliveira had suffered a leg injury and we were left with only three fit bowlers, Derek Underwood, Geoff Arnold and Tony Greig.

One person explained as Australia galloped to their victory. He was Ray Lindwall, the former Australian fast bowler, who was over in England covering the tour for a newspaper.

He had suffered a similar injury at one stage of his career and found he could not bowl properly either. Few people realise the essential part the left arm and hand play in the final stages of the delivery in the action of a right-arm fast bowler. The arm whips down and across the body helping to provide the momentum as the right arm comes up and over the top prior to the release of the ball. Every time I tried to whip that left arm down that morning, a searing pain shot up its whole length, causing me to lose my concentration and rhythm just when I needed it most.

Despite that I managed to finish with 24 wickets in the series, but that was seven behind Dennis Lillee, who took 31 and established a new record for an Australian in England. It was a great feat but I believe he suffered later as a result of being overbowled by Ian Chappell. Ian recognised that Dennis was going to be his match-winning bowler and used him as often as he could. Being the willing worker that he was, and enjoying the success he earned, Dennis never made a fuss.

Those 31 wickets were enough to comfort him through the aches and strains of the tour but they also turned him into a star performer. As such he was also overbowled when he returned home to play for Western Australia in the Sheffield Shield, and his back finally cracked under the pressure when Australia toured the Caribbean early in 1973. It was not really surprising that it would protest at some stage, for his action at the end of a long and punishing run threw great demands on his body.

Dennis has modified his action a little to ease that burden and he looks after himself far more carefully these days. The rise of Jeff Thomson has also eased the demands on him but, after talking to Dennis, I know he would have taken steps to protect himself even if he had lacked a regular opening partner.

The England dressing room was a very sober place at the end of that Oval Test match as we packed to go our separate ways while listening to the sounds of the Australian champagne celebrations in their dressing room almost directly overhead. Not only because we had failed to win the series.

Throughout that summer we all felt that we were taking part in a long drawn out farewell party. The time was drawing nearer when the old firm under Ray Illingworth was having to break up. Some of the older hands were getting towards the end of their Test careers and we realised it would probably be the last summer that the 1970–71 Ashes-winning side would be good enough at a Test level. The time was coming when new parts would have to be fitted.

The process started that winter when MCC were to tour India and Pakistan and Ray speeded it up himself by announcing he would not be available. Some people were upset by his decision and became further annoyed when I told the selectors I did not wish to be considered. Similar decisions came later from Geoff Boycott and John Edrich.

I thought hard and long before telling Alec Bedser I would not be available. The reason was purely medical. In 1969 in Pakistan with Colin Cowdrey's team I had caught a touch of dysentry – always a danger in that part of the world – and the after-affects were to stay with me for almost a year. In fact it took a month of taking pills in Australia to clear the final trace and I decided that, at that particular stage of my career, I was not going to expose myself to the danger of catching it again.

1973-75: Dropped again. Back for the Aussies

THE BREAKING up came earlier than I expected. Or Ray Illingworth expected for that matter. There were six Test matches during the 1973 summer, three against New Zealand and another three against the West Indies. I was dropped after the fourth Test. Ray found the axe falling around his neck after the final game when he was making plans for that winter's tour to the Caribbean.

I am sure that my sacking was a political move, forced on Ray at a time when he was struggling to hold on to the England leadership. His age had become a target for his critics. In fact he virtually told me in subsequent conversations that my omission was a "give and take" decision, although he did not expect to see me kept out of the Test scene for so long. I'm sure, too, that Ray's removal was a political manoeuvre inspired and pushed for by people who felt he was gaining too much power at their expense.

Both of us – along with Geoff Boycott – had chalked up a number of black marks against our names in the minds of many in authority because we spoke out and demanded a fair return and treatment for our efforts. I'm sure there was a feeling at Lord's and elsewhere that some senior players in the England dressing room were not coming to heel and needed to be taken down a peg or two. I was one of them.

Much of it can be traced back to the 1970–71 tour of Australia and I have since discovered that a meeting was held at Lord's after that tour to consider taking away the right of the England captain to sit in on selection committee meetings and have a vote. It was felt that Ray was winning too many battles in getting the players he wanted into the England side. The fact that he generally won the war as well, on the Test field, was not taken into consideration. After that tour Ray threatened all hell would break loose if any player lost his good conduct bonus as a result of what happened in Australia. That didn't happen, but Geoff Boycott and I had to report on orders from MCC for a dressing down by Billy Griffith.

In my own case I had a deep suspicion that my future Test life was to be short. That I was to be thrown overboard immediately I made a slip and could be ditched with some reasonable explanation.

As long as I kept taking wickets I was safe. If I missed out then I would be on the way out.

I did miss out in 1973 especially against New Zealand in the first half of the summer. Geoff Arnold took the wickets, the conditions helping his ability to make the ball swing. I should have taken more wickets than I did in the series for I often beat the batsman. It was disheartening. They just did not seem good enough to get a touch, and even Glenn Turner was the same that summer.

Sometimes it goes for you and sometimes it doesn't. It didn't go for me in 1973 but I was pleased for Geoff Arnold. In a way I was pleased for myself, for I thought we were a good combination, and that I had found a regular partner who could take some of the "striking" burden off my shoulders. He finished the three-match series with 16 wickets and he, too, might have had more. But Geoff and I were not seen as a partnership, and I'm sure my figures were measured against Geoff's. They suffered by comparison, and the way was open for me to be dropped.

Some critics recognised that I had bowled without much luck in the New Zealand series. Others pointed out that many of my 13 wickets had been down among the tail enders. The first Test against the West Indies at the Oval brought it all to a head. In the first innings I finished with nought for 71 and Geoff collected five wickets. Before the match was over I was being written off, said to be lethargic, bowling without my usual pace and fire. The criticism persisted even when I picked up the wickets of Rohan Kanhai, Clive Lloyd and Gary Sobers in the West Indies second innings.

That was the end for me until 1975 so far as Test matches are concerned. With the pressure going for me to be dropped, Ray eventually gave way when the selectors met to choose the side for the second Test against the West Indies. His own position was under fire and Ray felt it better to save the showdown argument over my presence until the time came to name the touring party for the MCC visit to the Caribbean that winter. He was hoping to be the captain, and he wanted me in the side.

Neither of us was to go with the team. Within minutes of the West Indies winning the final match at Lord's to take the series 2–0, Ray was informed that he had lost the England captaincy. My suspicions about his sacking were aroused when I heard later, from a source which should know, that even one the England selectors did not know that Ray had been replaced by Mike Denness. When the captaincy of the West Indies had been discussed over the weekend of that final Test at Lord's, Ray was still considered the first choice. This selector purported to be as surprised as most people to find Mike Denness had been invited to captain the tour instead!

Although the switch obviously ruled out Ray going to the West Indies, I might still have gone if Mike Denness had had his way. I understand he would have liked to have had me as one of his fast bowlers in the Caribbean and I know he wanted to take me back to Australia in 1974–75. Just before he attended a tour selection meeting Mike phoned me at home and asked me if I was prepared to go to Australia and he has since confirmed that he asked for me but everybody around the table was against it. That didn't surprise me. I said somewhere in a newspaper article that 1974 summer that the selectors would have to be shot before I made a Test comeback. I think my assessment was right.

From the time of Mike's appointment and the suggestion that I might go to the West Indies in 1973–74 some people expressed the fear that the combination might not work, that I might be an embarrassment to him because he could not control me. I do not know what they thought I would get up to.

There had also been a suggestion that Mike and I did not get along too well because I always seemed to save something special for him whenever Kent and Sussex played and usually claimed his wicket. There were no grounds for that suggestion at all.

It has also been suggested that Alec Bedser wasn't too keen to have me on the tour of Australia in 1974–75 when he was manager. There might well have been an element of truth in that, for I know his brother Eric, when asked for his views on the tour at the Oval one day towards the end of the 1974 summer, was overheard to say that I was not a good team man.

"Big Al" and I have not seen eye to eye on many matters over the years. He is of a different generation, brought up in an era where the professionals were still the work-horses, accepting orders and not questioning their masters. A big man who thrived on work, he had endless stamina, a nice easy action and would bowl all day and night if anybody asked him to. He had an intense love of the game.

Young cricketers in Alec's day still travelled to work on a bus and tube instead of arriving in cars as they do today. There was no chance then of cricketers adding to their income with outside interests. In those days no questions were asked, everybody knew his station in life. I think it still amazes Alec that younger people today are prepared to get up and challenge some of the things they are asked to do.

Whatever his views, he was certainly a party to the decision which seemed to have put an end to my Test career in 1973. I never really thought of it as the end. I said so at the time. I was only 32, had no weight problems, and had recovered my zest and zeal after a winter of rest instead of going to India and Pakistan.

previous page: John Snow, professional fast bowler (*Patrick Eagar*)

John Snow batting for Christ's Hospital School Colts (*The Times*)

John Snow receiving his county cap from Ted Dexter. Ken Suttle applauding (*Evening Argus*, *Brighton*)

John Snow's first Test wicket. J.R. Reid (New Zealand) caught by Jim Parks for 21, Lord's, 1965 (*Sport and General Press Agency, London*)

above: John Snow and Ken Higgs after their last wicket stand of 128 against West Indies, fifth Test, Oval, 1966. They were asked by the authorities to swap their beer for tea for the photographer (*Central Press Photos*, *London*)
right above: The Nawab of Pataudi, one-time captain of Sussex, batting for India. John Murray is keeping wicket (*Sport and General Press Agency, London*)
right below: Barry Richards, who might have joined Sussex rather than Hampshire (*Patrick Eagar*)

Grass roots cricket in Barbados (*Patrick Eagar*)

below: Basil d'Oliveira, thanked for the MCC tour of Pakistan, 1968–69, by the official tour brochure. Rodney Marsh is keeping wicket (*Patrick Eagar*)
bottom: Tear gas and police quelling the riot at Sabina Park, Kingston, on the 1967–68 tour (*Mrs Pauline Johnston*)
right: Away from it all. John Snow, fisherman (*Syndication International, London*)

far left: John Snow's hundredth 'Test' wicket. Mike Procter (Rest of the World) bowled at Lord's, 1970
left: Gary Sobers, greatest-ever all-rounder, bowling for the West Indies in the Oval Test match of 1973 (*Patrick Eagar*)

Melbourne. On this day in 1975, Australia v West Indies, over 85,000 spectators packed the ground (*Patrick Eagar*)

Incidents which led to Illingworth leading the England team from the field in the final Test at Sydney, 1971. Below, John Snow is grabbed by a spectator after (right) a ball from him hit Terry Jenner on the head (*Central Press Photos, London*)

John Snow knocks over Sunil Gavaskar in the infamous collision at Lord's during the Test match with India in 1971 (*Sport and General Press Agency, London*)

left: Seymour Nurse, rated by John Snow as one of the hardest batsmen to dismiss, batting for West Indies at Trent Bridge, 1966. Colin Cowdrey is at slip (*Central Press Photos, London*)
above: Andy Roberts (left) and Dennis Lillee (right). John Snow believes both lost some effectiveness at stages in their careers through being overbowled (*Patrick Eagar*)

left: Alec Bedser, chairman of the English Test selectors (*Sport and General Press Agency, London*)
below: Colin Milburn batting against the West Indies in 1966. 'Ollie' was a great loss to English cricket when an eye injury ended his Test career (*Central Press Photos, London*)
right: Mike Griffith, Sussex captain, batting against Surrey. Arnold Long, later a Sussex player himself, is behind the stumps (*Patrick Eagar*)

Ian Chappell on his way to a century for Australia against England at the Oval, 1972. Alan Knott is the wicket keeper (*Patrick Eagar*)

Greg Chappell, who took over from brother Ian as Australia's captain in 1975 (*Patrick Eagar*)

opposite: Tony Greig, captain of Sussex and later of England, in action against Australia at Perth in 1974 (*Patrick Eagar*)
left: Clive Lloyd, captain of West Indies, during his century in the first World Cup final at Lord's (*Patrick Eagar*)
below: John Snow stumped Marsh bowled Inverarity for 48, England v Australia, Headingley, 1972 (*Patrick Eagar*)

The Sussex County Cricket Ground at Hove

right: Ray Illingworth hooks and Gary Sobers and Deryck Murray flinch in the England v West Indies Test at the Oval, 1973. The ball, arrowed, is on its way to the ropes. Illingworth, England captain, was much respected by his fellow players (*Patrick Eagar*)
below: Part of Derek Underwood's close-catching field at Headingley in the 1972 Test against Australia. Inverarity is caught by Illingworth (*Patrick Eagar*)
below right: David Steele, England hero of 1975, on his way to a century for Northants against Middlesex at Lord's, 1976 (*Central Press Photos, London*)

Alan Knott and John Snow jubilant as Rodney Marsh is bowled, England v Australia, Headingley, 1975 (*Patrick Eagar*)

I knew that I would be back at some stage. Possibly not as a regular bowler for a full series but rather for the occasional match, in the way that Middlesex's John Price popped up from time to time when injury problems arose.

The one chance of finishing the 1973 summer on a high note came with Sussex's appearance in the Gillette Cup final at Lord's – our fifth appearance in the eleven years of the competition. Unhappily it was to be our third successive final defeat when Gloucestershire were inspired by a brutal innings by Mike Procter and went on to win by 40 runs.

That was a big disappointment, but the saddest match of the year had come at the earlier end of the 1973 summer when Ray and I – having turned down the India and Pakistan tour – were made to prove ourselves by taking part in the first of the revived Test trials.

The selectors, particularly Alec Bedser, seem to place a lot of store in these games. I find them a bore and an insult. I concede they do give the selectors a chance of seeing all the main Test contenders together, but selections should never be made on the happenings in one match. I cannot see the point of having proven players such as Geoff Boycott, John Edrich, Alan Knott and others in these trials. Everything anybody wants to know about senior players is known and their places should go to youngsters on the fringe of selection. The selectors have often complained that they do not get the time to study all the players they want. They waste an opportunity by insisting on the tried and trusted taking part in a trial match.

That is how I felt when I was again selected for the second trial at Worcester early in the 1974 season. I didn't particularly want to play. I knew it was not going to prove anything in my case. My record spoke for itself. If it wasn't good enough, a three-day game at Worcester wasn't going to make any difference.

Geoff Boycott and John Edrich proved the point in that game. Geoff killed it stone dead by scoring a century in each innings, even though he reckoned he was out of touch at the start of the match. If Geoff helped to kill the match, John Edrich hammered the nails in the coffin by replying with a century in the first innings for the Rest and 90 in the second. What that match proved I have no idea. Except that Geoff and John were the two most reliable batsmen in the country. Surprise, surprise.

The player I felt sorry for at Worcester was Frank Hayes, who started his Test career in remarkable fashion with a century against the West Indies at the Oval in 1973, but then suffered mixed fortunes including a disappointing tour of the West Indies.

Here was a player with great potential fighting to make an impression in order to regain his Test place and I had to laugh on the last afternoon when Ossie Wheatley, the former Glamorgan player who was then a Test selector, came into the dressing room where Frank was waiting to bat. I had already expressed my views about Test trials to Jackie Bond, one of the other selectors, so why stop there.

There was no chance of an outright result after two and a half days devoted to Boycott and Edrich. Nevertheless Ossie came into our dressing room and said: "Come on, have a go. Try and make a game of it."

I could not hold back my chuckle which had Ossie turning round and snapping: "You can cut out the sniggering." I replied that if any player needed to play decently and properly, building an innings in the right way to show he was Test material, it was Frank. Yet here was a selector suggesting that he went in and threw his bat around in one-day cavalier fashion, the type of cricket they claim is ruining Test match players. It was unbelievable.

Wisely Frank ignored Ossie's suggestion and played sensibly when his turn came to bat. It might not have done him any good if he had followed the advice. Before his innings it was reported that some selectors had been seen leaving.

When selected for a Test trial there is little else to do but turn up and play. Playing for the MCC is a different matter. That is separate. I declined the invitation in 1975 when asked to play against the Australians. It smacked of a form of Test trial and I just was not interested, especially after I had played for England in the Prudential World Cup.

Jack Bailey, the MCC secretary, must have been on the phone to my home for more than half an hour trying to persuade me to change my mind when I first turned the invitation down. I kept asking him why he was so keen for me to play without getting a direct answer. I imagine the selectors wanted to have a look at me bowling against the Australians in a three-day match before deciding whether I was still capable of producing the goods in a Test match as opposed to a one-day game.

I was having nothing to do with it. I felt that I did not need to go on trial to prove anything and the place could have been better used by the selectors having a look at one of the younger bowlers.

It was largely because I felt the younger and less experienced players were getting a bit of a raw deal that I ran into trouble on yet another tour – that of South Africa with Derrick Robins' team led by Brian Close late in 1973.

By the end of the tour I was disappointed with the whole arrangement and the way a certain elite band of players seemed to have all the privileges. As one of the senior Test players with the party I could have enjoyed those privileges but that would have caused greater embarrassment for some of the others. The question of cars became a troublesome one. A firm loaned the party two or three cars wherever we went but the so-called lesser lights never seemed to be able to get one when they wanted to go out.

More importantly I felt that the tour was run too much like a Test exercise. Derrick Robins, who has now settled in South Africa after serving Warwickshire cricket and Coventry City Football Club, was naturally keen to win because the performances of the side would increase its standing. Brian Close was obviously keen to win for that is his way. And I certainly don't like losing. Yet I felt we placed too much emphasis on getting results when we were a private tour party.

Not until we came up against the South African Invitation XI in games billed as "mini Tests" were we really extended in any way, yet we always seemed to be fielding the strongest side, which limited the opportunities of Kent all-rounder Graham Johnson, Essex left-arm spinner Ray East and Lancashire opening bowler Peter Lee. East, in fact, bowled only nine first-class overs on the tour and Johnson and Lee played in only half the first-class matches. On two of those occasions Lee played only because Australian Test spinner John Gleeson went down injured.

I thought this was all wrong. It was the type of tour from which all three would have benefited had they been given a chance. They were relatively inexperienced cricketers and a healthy dose of cricket in South Africa would surely have improved their chances of making the England side. Perhaps I was remembering my own experiences and what a season on South African wickets did for me back in the winter of 1965–66, when I had been left out of the MCC side for Australia.

In Johannesburg, the setting for the final of the three "mini Tests," I became disgruntled with the whole organisation and finally pinched the keys to one car. It caused a bit of an upset and I was soon told to return the keys.

That evening a team meeting was arranged to discuss details for the final big match starting the next day. Before then I had arranged to have a drink with a friend in the hotel bar. I kept that appointment and during our talk I completely forgot the time. It wasn't until 15 minutes or so after the team meeting had been scheduled to start that I was reminded, when my room-mate John Lever was sent to get me. He knew I must be still in the bar.

I told John I'd be at the meeting as soon as I had finished my drink. Feeling sore after the morning episode, I didn't hurry, and by the time I'd finished the drink the meeting was almost over. I saw no point in joining it at such a late stage.

The next thing I knew I'd been dropped from the team. Closey, Derrick Robins, tour manager Les Ames and John Murray, the four selectors, took my absence from the meeting as a deliberate snub. Naturally I apologised to Derrick Robins and explained my feelings about what had happened but the decision had already been made by then.

They stuck to it even when Brian Close decided the following morning he wanted me after all and tried to get me back in the side. It was a pity because we lost the game – the only defeat on the tour – when Eddie Barlow scored a double century, Lee Irvine, once of Essex, scored a century and their total of 528 for eight proved enough to get home by an innings and 83 runs with a day to spare.

My Test recall in 1975 was memorable if for one reason only, that of seeing the look of absolute joy on the face of Northamptonshire's David Steele as he went from one triumph to another after being given the chance to represent his country at the age of 33. If there was one man who got his share of pleasure during that summer it was "Stainless." He lived in Wonderland from the second Test onwards even if he was not everybody's idea of Alice.

Nobody who was in the England dressing room at the time will ever forget his entry into Test cricket as a batsman during the second Test. Not just for the runs he scored when England were 49 for four, but for the walk he took out to the middle. "Stainless" lost his way. Just as I had done on my first appearance at Lord's back in that 1963 Gillette Cup final.

On all his previous visits to the ground with Northants he had gone to the crease from the visitors' dressing room. This time he was in the home dressing room, the one used by Middlesex. There is hardly any difference in the journey from the door, down two flights of stairs and out through the Long Room – except that everything is reversed.

When the first wicket went, Barry Wood falling leg before against Dennis Lillee, up stood "Stainless" and off he went. Unfortunately he looked for the door on the right at the bottom of the staircase instead of the left, and got lost. Meanwhile out in the middle everybody waited for "Stainless" to appear little knowing that inside he was frantically extricating himself from the gentleman's toilet in the basement having gone down two flights of stairs too many.

With his greying hair and glasses he is an unlikely looking athletic hero and I think this is partly the reason the English public took to him, especially those watching at home on television who were not avid followers of the sport. I think the whole country felt for him when he just missed his first Test century at Headingley that summer. Even the Australians did, and they don't give anything away.

The more successful he became as the summer wore on the more I heard spectators wonder why the England selectors had waited until he was approaching the autumn of his career before turning him into an overnight success. It is a good question, and there is no real answer.

Perhaps a change in the selection system might be helped with the appointment of a "Mr Cricket" or a full-time selector for the summer months only. The Cricket Committee of the Test and County Cricket Board suggested this in the winter of 1973 to establish a tighter relationship between players and the administration.

The formation of the selection committee has changed since I first got my chance in the England side. Back in the middle 1960s it consisted of former players in Doug Insole, Alec Bedser, Peter May and Cyril Washbrook. All part-timers and unpaid, giving up their free time in the summer in order to do their "scouting" work. The only "gain", apart from the prestige of being a selector, was the possibility of combining business trips with trips to look at players.

Gradually the make-up was changed when it was decided it was better to have at least one active player on the selection committee – apart from the captain – to provide another view. A player can study the game and the candidates from the best possible vantage point, out in the middle. Style, ability and class can be determined from the pavilion balcony but not temperament and nerves.

Don Kenyon, the former Worcestershire and England opening batsman, was the first of these playing selectors, followed by Alan Smith of Warwickshire, Jack Bond of Lancashire and Brian Taylor of Essex. Ray Illingworth might have been one as well when he was put forward after his sacking as England captain. Unfortunately his name did not go the full way. He was rejected presumably because some on the TCCB felt he was too close to the players. I would have thought that that was just the type of person needed.

If Ray had been on the committee, or if England had had a supremo using captains, senior players and umpires as a sounding board, David Steele might have been given a chance some two or three seasons earlier. I know there was a time when Ray Illingworth seriously considered his claims after we returned from Australia.

It was interesting that, following our defeat at Edgbaston by Australia, both Ray and Brian Close went into print urging the selectors to pick Steele. They suggested he had the qualifications to hold his own against Dennis Lillee and Jeff Thomson on English wickets at least. He was very much the "players' choice" when he was picked for the second Test at Lord's.

I regarded him as an annoying so-and-so whenever I played against him. I always fancied myself to get him out because he has often looked so limited as a batsman. But usually I still found him in, left leg down the track, nudging his ones and twos long after I had been taken off. The fact that he has looked a limited player has been deceptive. He has carefully analysed his game, decided exactly what he can and cannot do, come to terms with himself and played within those limitations.

He is blessed, of course, by having strong powers of concentration which enable him to go steadily along at the same rate, batting it out under difficult conditions when other batsmen have given up the fight and succumbed to a moment of rashness. This is vitally important in Test cricket.

When it comes to playing at the highest level I am a great believer in selecting people who can put their house in order mentally, even if they do not possess the pure cricketing ability of some others. There are a great many players – batsmen and bowlers alike – who look the part in the nets, in practice matches and out in the middle when the going is easy, but who crumble when the pressure is on. I am sure this is where Charlie Elliot, the former Test umpire, has been a great help since joining the selection panel. He knows the ones who crack.

In past years a number of selectors have looked for the Ted Dexters, the Peter Mays and the Colin Cowdreys of this world, players who look the part technically with grace, timing and power, plus a full range of strokes. They have been disappointed when such players have not been able to produce the goods in the tension and atmosphere created by a full house at Lord's, Melbourne or Sabina Park, Jamaica.

The workers have provided the backbone of England's batting over the years: Ken Barrington, John Edrich, Geoff Boycott, Basil D'Oliveira and even Alan Knott. They have not been the easiest on the eye at times as they have patiently played a dead bat to the good balls and waited for the loose deliveries to punish. In the Test match arena when the bowler is supposed to be the best of his type the loose deliveries do not come often and even greater powers of concentration are needed.

These players very seldom let England down. They score a century a series, possibly two, and are always chipping in with their fifties and sixties. Their contribution at the end can be measured in runs and not memories. They are more successful than, say, a Keith Fletcher who possesses greater natural ability and power but has not produced the weight of runs expected of him at a Test level.

I know the type of player I prefer to bowl against. I like those rated in the genius class, and not only for the challenge such contests bring. If the batsman is willing to attack and chance his arm he is obviously presenting you with a greater opportunity to snatch his wicket. There will be more occasions when you might be able to deceive him and tempt him into error.

Although Geoff Boycott and I came into the game round about the same time I have not bowled against him for Sussex against Yorkshire as often as many people imagine. Many of the battles we have had have been off the field. In a friendly, mickey-taking sort of way. Geoff is very good at kidding people along, getting them worked up and over-anxious by telling them exactly what he is going to do to them once he faces them on the field.

I can well remember one match at Hove when the rest of the Yorkshire team gave him plenty of stick because he succeeded in rubbing me up the wrong way during play. Before the match Geoff had his usual go, a batsman's version of the way Fred Trueman went into the visiting dressing room on the morning of the match to warn the opposition what he was going to do to them.

Geoff, I believe, had taken a century off Sussex the previous summer and when he saw me before the start of play he called out: "I'll take another century off you today, Snowey. Just wait until I get going." As it happened Yorkshire batted first and soon after their innings started Geoff drove me through the covers. It was going for two runs and I had already turned my back on Boycott when he started off on his first run. As he passed me he gave me a playful pat on the legs with his bat. At least I suppose it was meant to be playful but it was quite a rap. I was a little annoyed and as Boycott put his bat down behind the crease ready to start his second run, I kicked it away so that he stumbled. The umpire was amazed; he wasn't sure what was going on.

The incident was enough to get me going, and I worked up some extra pace. I can clearly recall the startled look on Phil Sharpe's face as a couple whistled past him before I got him out. The same thing happened to Jackie Hampshire. Later Don Wilson told me the Yorkshire boys gave Boycott a going over when he was eventually out, having told him beforehand that the last thing he must do was to upset me. Such is the strange power of a fast bowler.

As a conversation piece people have frequently asked me which of my many wickets has given me the most pleasure. They expect I will pluck one from Australia or West Indies. Or perhaps a match-winning effort in a Test at home. Before 1975 no ready answer sprang to mind.

Now I no longer stop to think. My answer does not concern one wicket but three. Those of Alan Turner and the Chappell brothers, Ian and Greg. I took them when England played Australia at Lord's in the second Test that summer. I felt each one proved a point. That I was not over the hill as a Test fast bowler despite having been ignored for eight Test matches at home and two tours abroad. Each of these three batsmen was well beaten by a good delivery, two out leg before and Ian Chappell caught behind. Down at fine leg after that opening spell I bloody nearly cried.

What is wrong with cricket organisation

In some quarters in cricket professionalism is still regarded as a dirty word. It is a word conviently used to explain any supposed scar or blemish on the game caused by cricketers either demanding more – and I don't just mean in a monetary sense – or being involved in an incident on the field. The passing of the amateur, particularly as a leader, is still mourned by a few who regarded "the fancy hats" as the only ones qualified to know how to play the game in the right spirit.

Yet I have always found that cricketers – professional or otherwise – are basically a very level-headed lot whether they are club cricketers toiling away on the village green at the grass roots of the sport or those earning their living at the highest level. They do not make a noise unless they have a valid point to make and usually their love for the game and its well-being is as strong, if not stronger, than that of those who pass judgement on them.

Many people will be surprised to know that cricketers from two county clubs came near to refusing to play on two separate issues during the 1975 summer because they felt they were not getting a fair hearing from their employers. Worcestershire players went so far as to inform their committee of their intention of downing bats unless they were given an early promise that their frustrations and long drawn out differences would be aired. I understand that only a last minute dash by Jimmy James, the Lancashire secretary, averted a similar situation when Lancashire were on the point of striking.

Worcestershire's troubles burst into the open in the autumn and ended with a public meeting during which hundreds of supporters turned up to air their views. In fact it took two chaotic meetings to resolve the problem, because with many unable to get in to the first the club was forced reluctantly to hire the largest hall in the county for another. I say reluctantly because the secretary claimed the club could not afford a second meeting and was only shamed into agreement by a member who volunteered to pay the costs in order to discover the background to the players' unrest. The results were the reorganisation of Worcestershire's cumbersome committee and the settling of the players' problems. Until 1975 the Worcestershire committee was 54 strong of which only 15 were elected. It has now been reduced to 22 members of whom 15 are still elected. The running of the club should benefit.

The Lancashire issue came to a head in high summer when three of their England players, Barry Wood, Peter Lever and Frank Hayes, dropped out of a first team match on the morning of a game against Derbyshire.

I will not comment on the issues involved. That is not my concern. But, after talking to the players themselves, I am convinced that both disputes could have been solved long before the affairs became public and bitterness inflamed the feelings of both sides. In each case I can fault the county organisation on the grounds of attitude and approach. That is particularly surprising in the case of Lancashire, who have built up a reputation among players over the last half a dozen years as one of the more progressive and enlightened of the county clubs.

The county's dispute with the players began at the end of the 1974 season and was still not solved when the players reported back for the start of the 1975 campaign, although the players tell me that negotiations had reached a stage where settlement appeared to be only a matter of days away. Eventually they expected it to be sorted out and resolved at the June monthly meeting of the particular committee involved. It wasn't, and that was the breaking point for the players. Their frustration turned into anger when they discovered that the matter had been put back to July, the June meeting being cancelled because the committee members wanted to watch the Benson and Hedges quarter-final at Leicestershire.

The Lancashire players believed, quite rightly in my opinion, that with the dispute causing internal unrest the committee should have met on another day in June instead of waiting till the following month. Or, alternatively, the meeting could have been held at Leicestershire as the members were present watching the quarter-final. Lancashire were the losers in the end. Although the players were forbidden to speak, the news leaked out, and the club had unfavourable publicity as well as the damage to the previously good relations between the committee and the staff to contend with.

Worcestershire were the losers in their case too. The net result of their dispute was the loss of essential players which left them short of strength for the 1976 season. Brian Brain, Jim Yardley, Rod Cass and John Parker were regular first team players who left the club as a result of the clash, and the relationship between the remaining players and their employers was further damaged.

I believe Yorkshire's struggles during the first half of the 1970s can be traced to another case of a wrong and mistaken attitude on the part of the club. This cost them the services of Ray Illingworth after the end of the 1968 season – a departure that started to break up the side that had proved the outstanding team of the previous eight years.

Ray, of course, has no reason to regret the switch from being Yorkshire's all-rounder to Leicestershire's captain. It is doubtful whether he would ever have captained England if he had stayed with his native county. But despite the personal success he has enjoyed in recent years and his admiration for the organisation at Leicestershire, I have a sneaking suspicion he would have preferred to end his playing days with the county of his birth.

The dispute involved Ray's determination to seek some extra security after spending the best years of his life serving the county. Yorkshire at the time employed their players on a year-to-year basis, although this was done on trust and they could, if they wanted, give a player one month's notice. Ray was looking for a longer contract – a three-year term of employment being his ideal. It seems a not outlandish request for England's top off-spinner, who was still engaged in Test cricket and had some years ahead of him in the game.

Stubbornly Yorkshire refused. Obviously Ray's age had some bearing on the issue, and they had another younger off-spinner in the background in Geoff Cope. But Ray refused to back down, willingly accepted Leicestershire's offer of a three-year contract – one of several made to him – and in 1976, some eight years later, he was still signing three year contracts.

Yorkshire cannot possibly claim to have won that battle. The team was never the same without Ray and before long Yorkshire themselves were offering young players longer contracts in order to keep them.

All three instances I have quoted portray an attitude still prevalent in first-class cricket – the old question of them and us. Many counties show a lack of man-management without which none can possibly hope to find success. And ultimately it is the players who are made to suffer. That is the greatest tragedy of all.

Management is not just a question of finding suitable players but of looking after them. The county clubs who have managed to do this have reaped the benefit in recent years.

Leicestershire is a perfect example. The attitude has been on the right lines, and management on a high level thanks to Mike Turner as secretary/manager. Mike, a former player, knows and understands players, and treats them as equals, allowing them to have their say, and to make suggestions. The players are lucky with Ray Illingworth to guide them and Mike Turner to help fight for their rights.

Kent is another such club and perhaps it is not just an accident that they also employed a manager/secretary who was a former player in Les Ames. They have a healthy following, perhaps the most biased crowd in the country, but the respect of those supporters had to be earned, and it was the players who had to earn it. Kent are fortunate to have Colin Page, another former player, to take over the managership from Les Ames and carry on his revival work.

I can quote more. Essex, for example, where Doug Insole, once of England, has been instrumental in getting the county organised to make a profit in years when larger, more wealthy clubs were suffering almost crippling losses.

It is when I look at a county such as Essex – where Doug Insole has been not too proud to take off his jacket to arrange deck chairs, take money, sell scorecards and do many other small tasks – that I feel so frustrated when I take another look nearer home and see Sussex. Sussex should be one of the foremost counties in the country, magnificently equipped, well supported and with a string of honours after the name. Sadly, it isn't.

Only recently, since Tony Croel-Rees took over the chair at Sussex, have I felt that the club has been moving in the right direction, with a more positive and far-seeing leadership at the top to match the new spirit emerging on the field. Unfortunately it has come at a time when inflation is hitting everybody which makes it harder to catch up after the many wasted years in more moneyed times when the club just drifted along.

At the last count there were 37 elected heads on the council from which 15 Executive Committee members are chosen. And that, I am convinced, has been the root cause of the problems in Sussex over the years. Under half that number should be sufficient to run a county organisation on smooth lines, with the help of experts ready to lend advice in any field the committee wanted.

Throughout most of my time I have felt a gulf between the players and committee and I have already given some examples earlier in the book when discussing Sussex's lack of success. There has also been a gulf between the committee and spectators. Too often the spectators have been treated as though they should regard it as a privilege to pay their money to get in. The spectators have received very little encouragement.

Hove should rank as one of the finest grounds in the country. Instead it is hemmed in so that development is restricted. In the past, the county club owned some of the surrounding sites but allowed them to pass out of their control. They have also missed the opportunity to buy other houses which could have been knocked down and the ground and facilities expanded. This lack of foresight has lost the opportunity of building, say, a leisure complex, which could have been used summer and winter, day and evening for many indoor sports. A centre on the Edgbaston style – only better – for the whole of Brighton and Hove to use, giving the county cricket organisation a real identity in a lively seaside resort as well as providing money to keep the club running smoothly and healthily today. That is a far-off dream now. A potted development history shows what I mean.

Former committee members have told me that plans were drawn up 20 or so years ago to re-site the present pavilion which was considered to be inadequate. The idea was to rebuild it at the top end of the ground, and to increase the size to allow more members to obtain a view of the match from behind the bowler's arm.

Incredibly, I'm told, the plan was rejected because some members of the main committee felt it would be an act of sacrilege to pull down the steps that had been walked down by such players as C.B. Fry, Duleepsinhji, Vine and others. Instead some £35,000 was spent on patching up the present pavilion – money wasted for the building is unsuitable for the present day.

On another occasion the chance arose to build a larger public house complete with flats and restaurant on land next to the present public house situated by the main entrance to the ground. Apparently, that was defeated by one vote.

At one time the ground did boast of a small sports complex of sorts. Unfortunately it was sold and became a factory. It came up for sale again but the club did nothing and now large blocks of flats shadow the ground. It is true the Gilligan Stand came out of the development, but this is an updated "cowshed" of a building compared to what might have been. It has provided new indoor nets but largely the space is wasted. The spectators cannot be too happy about it either. The roof slopes from back to front and they have constantly to stop their seats sliding forward.

The club did erect a new squash centre at the top end of the ground in 1974. Unfortunately the appointed architect left a gap between the floors and walls which traps the ball. One member even fell over and found his racquet stuck in the gap. There was no bar in which he could have improved his temper. A bar is essential for a building of that type and one is now being added. At a greater cost, of course.

A lack of understanding of the human being on the Sussex committee is shown by the way they have treated some of the players. The ending of Ken Suttle's contract in 1970 was a disgraceful episode. Ken heard about it in the most casual way, when Eddie Harrison, then chairman of the cricket committee, caught him walking up the roadway at the back of the pavilion. Ken later told me the news came in the following manner: "Hello Ken, I've been meaning to have a word with you. How's the wife and family? All right I hope. Oh, by the way, you're not being re-engaged for next season." Ken was, understandably, left speechless.

The whole set up at Hove is geared to breed inefficiency because of the way the council is elected. The county is divided into areas and the members in those areas are allowed to vote representatives on the council – the number of representatives from each area depending on the size of membership. Midhurst and Petworth area, for instance, can vote two people on the 37-strong council as there are 58 members in that part of the county.

I believe the whole system should be reorganised to make sure we have the most suitable people put forward to take on committee work. Certainly not the lady member who wishes the players to walk around the ground selling ice cream and chatting to the crowd when not batting or fielding. I know we wear white but that is unbelievable.

I wish to avoid having on the committee the ex-player who cannot tell one player from another. He was at the ground one day watching the game when Michael Buss was bowled. Soon afterwards he met Tony Buss who was on his way to the secretary's office.

"What happened there Michael?" asked the committeeman. "Did the ball move late?"

"I don't know," replied Tony acidly. "My name is Peter Graves."

Michael and Tony may be brothers but there is no difficulty telling which is which.

In fact one attempt was made by a splinter group at an annual general meeting to revamp the club, but the late Duke of Norfolk, who was President, declared it was out of order and closed the proceedings.

Mention of His Grace reminds me of another mistaken identity case during a game against Kent. The Duke was talking to Colin Cowdrey when Peter Graves walked past. Peter was in earshot long enough to hear the following snatch of the conversation.

Duke: "Is that one of your players, Colin?"

Kipper: "No, your Grace. He's Peter Graves, one of yours."

Despite the Duke's out-of-order ruling, I still think the club should be reorganised to allow men with vision and ideas to flourish instead of being held back by penny pinching and conservatism. The old maxim that you have speculate to accumulate held good 30 years ago and does so today.

A lack of drive and ambition at the top of any organisation soon spreads downwards and leads to inefficiency. It can be seen through some of the appointments Sussex have made over the years.

How, for instance, could anybody make Jim Parks (snr) coach of a professional club when he was 60 years of age or thereabouts? This is not a criticism of him personally. He is a fine man, and a very nice and pleasant person to talk to, but the age gap was far too large for him to be able actively to associate and communicate with the number of teenagers coming to the club.

The same argument applies to other appointments of secretaries. Again this is not a criticism of the people actually employed, who have often done the job to the best of their ability. It has been obvious though that the county has engaged unsuitable people simply because they have not been prepared to spend money on wages to attract the best. The club has had the habit of seeking pensioned civil servants and ex-officers from the services. People who have been looking for £2,000 or so a year to supplement their pensions. This is not the way to run a business, and cricket is an entertainment business.

For this last reason I believe the running of the Sussex County Cricket Club should be divided between two separate bodies. There are two sides of the problem: the financial side, finding the money to pay the players, maintain and develop the ground and invest for the future, and the playing side, the business of winning championships and cups in the middle.

Surely the best method is to have experts in each field running the show. Three or four proven businessmen with an interest in sport should be given the responsibility for looking after the financial side of things with a brief to make money. Their job would be to run the club on purely business-like lines, profit being the only motive and their influence should end once they have made the money and organised the club on a sound financial footing.

The playing side should again be run by the accepted experts, former players, in conjunction with the captain and senior professionals. They, in turn, would not be allowed to interfere with the commercial side of the organisation.

All this is very much, if you like, the way sponsors are involved in cricket at the moment. Benson and Hedges, John Player, Prudential and Gillette put up the money but their responsibility ends at that point. How the money is used in the various competitions and the running of the competitions are left with the Test and County Cricket Board, the experts on the playing front.

Such a two-tier system could not arise at Sussex under the present system. Getting business expertise is such a hit-and-miss affair with the current method of voting people on to the council, and there are far too many people involved who lack an intimate knowledge of cricket and cricketers.

I may have sounded harsh on Sussex but I write as I have found over the years. Sussex have been picked out because my experience has been with the club and for no other reasons. From my conversations with other cricketers, the complaints I have made with regard to Sussex apply equally to many other counties. In almost all of them there has been a lack of foresight in their planning, a lack of expertise and vision in the way the club has been run. The price is being paid today. The result is a constant struggle to make ends meet to provide a decent wage to attract the right talent into the game, and to provide comfort and decent amenities for spectators and persuade them to return.

A few pages back I mentioned that the situation had improved at Hove lately with Tony Croel-Rees becoming chairman. He has the strength of personality and the aggression needed to drive through some of the "sandbagging" that has held up Sussex over the years.

Other counties, too, seem to have found some strong men, and conditions of employment have improved in many county clubs. The financial rewards have got better but often they are still short of being a decent living wage especially for the county player who will never be good enough to play Test cricket and pick up some of the perks that go with being a star man. Geoff Greenidge recently returned to the West Indies because he was fed up with being constantly on the bread line and I know two other Sussex players have seriously considered giving up the game for the same reason. Strange as it may seem to some, cricketers do need money to exist, but when former Sussex wicket-keeper Alan Mansell asked secretary Arthur Dumbrell about a salary increase he was told: "You don't worry about money at your age, do you? Surely you play to enjoy yourself."

The situation has been improved on a national level with the formation and the growth of influence of the Professional Cricketers Association under the guidance of Jack Bannister, the former Warwickshire bowler. Another main improvement has come from the switch in power from the MCC to the Test and County Cricket Board, who are now responsible and accountable for the running of the game in England.

There has been a more progressive attitude emanating from the men who form the Test and County Cricket Board than there ever seemed to be from the MCC. More "liberal" men are getting into positions of influence and there has been a dialogue between the PCA and the TCCB that was missing before. An avenue of communication has been established that has led to an improvement in the players' lot and a greater awareness on the part of those making decisions of how the players feel. The authorities are realising that the players DO care how the game is played and run and what happens in the future. And that, perhaps, players should be heard as well as seen.

It is still not right. The money problem has not been solved and the freedom of the players is still limited. It always will be while they have to rely on benefit seasons to give them any lasting reward for their service. Benefits are a form of blackmail which many clubs have exploited in the past. All players, that is regular first-team players with a county, have had to live with the threat that unless they behaved themselves, spoke when spoken to and obeyed the rules, their one giant pay day would be threatened, for they cannot change clubs while registration rules necessitate a two-year requalification period elsewhere.

These faults are not just confined to English cricket. It is the same overseas – indeed often worse – judging from my own experiences. But the effect has been emphasised in England because it is the only country where players actually earn their living out in the middle and do not play cricket only for sport or as a sideline.

That pattern is changing quite rapidly, speeded up by the entry of overseas players into English county cricket, "mercenaries" playing full time. In Australia there are now full-time cricketers whose whole income is tied up with their playing the game. All these players are showing greater concern about the way the game is run in their own country.

I am sure this is the reason behind some of the recent flare-ups and controversies surrounding former captain Ian Chappell – regarded as a great leader one day but loud, uncouth and dangerous the next by the very same critics. Loud because he is a trendy dresser with a liking for vivid colours and unconventional styles in clothes. Uncouth because he ignores some of the game's traditional ways. Dangerous because he stands up for his point of view. The point is that Ian Chappell has become frustrated by the way cricket has been handled. He resents the large profits gathered in by the Australian Board of Control in recent years and the poor share handed over to the people who have made these profits possible – the players.

He feels it is wrong that players can be penalised for serving their country as Dennis Lillee has been. On his return from touring England in 1975 Dennis was told he had lost his job because his employers could not afford to have him away for months at a time. He is not the only one to have suffered over the years. Usually two or three members of any Australian touring party find they do not have a job to return to.

Players from Western Australia are usually hardest hit. They are such a long way from the main populace that they have to use their holidays to join the month long Eastern State tour of Queensland,

New South Wales and Victoria during which Western Australia play their away games. There is no opportunity for the Western Australia Test players to save up holidays to go on an overseas tour. It is not right that this situation should arise either at home or abroad when in most countries Test match profits are now so huge. The receipts for the Australia versus West Indies Tests in 1975–76 were a record $1,161,756.

I know that the Australian authorities were annoyed when Chappell made no attempt to prevent the players getting together and asking for more when they were in England in 1975. Some people have even suggested it was the end of his days as captain. He announced his own resignation but the word was that Australia would not appoint him again because he did not toe the official line. Possibly Chappell has overstepped the mark at times as I have been accused of doing in the past. I cannot say, not having seen his clashes with umpires and not being present at his arguments with the South Australian authorities. But I do know how Ian feels.

Cricket as a profession

WHEN I started mapping out the framework for this story I was a bachelor. Sometime during the writing of the last few chapters my status has changed and I am now a married man. With that change comes an admission on my part from deep down. I recognise that my lengthy touring days are probably over.

I have known my wife Jenny for many years and would undoubtedy have married long before this if I had been a bank clerk or lorry driver, or taken up my other career as a school teacher. Instead I deliberately put off the moment because the wife of a regular Test cricketer has a pretty rough time. It is an unfair partnership with the husband away half the summer and most winters, and with the lady of the house left behind to run the place, pay the bills, bring up the children and the rest. Several marriages of Test cricketers have struggled under the strain brought about by long periods of separation.

Touring is fun, rewarding and fascinating. We cricketers are given the opportunity of visiting places beyond our reach in normal circumstances because we have an ability which makes our sport our work. I have received many envious glances from friends and relations as I've boarded a plane at the first sign of winter and headed for some far away sun spot.

Touring can also be tough and very demanding: three to six months of constant packing and unpacking, living out of suitcases with home a succession of impersonal hotel rooms, some good, some bad, the majority indifferent. The tourist's life is in the open, with every move made under the spotlight of publicity. The television lens watches everything on the field, the curious eyes of strangers watch in hotels and streets, at receptions, cocktail parties and a succession of dinners. The moments of complete freedom are few and far between.

A touring party usually consists of sixteen players plus manager, assistant manager and physiotherapist, the last very important in keeping everybody in shape. I have been fortunate to travel with two excellent men in Jack Jennings of Northants and Bernard Thomas, who tends the wounded at Warwickshire. Generally it is a closely knit party, drawn together by the common aim of winning, sharing its moments of triumph and the periods of depression and disappointment. Yet one can still be incredibly lonely at times. There are odd nights when the wish is just to get away from everybody and forget there was ever a game called cricket.

Tours effect cricketers in so many ways. Some would be almost unrecognisable to their friends back home who think they know them well. There are the players who are the life and soul of the party at home but who become withdrawn, moping and miserable when separated from their families for a lengthy period. There are the quiet ones in England who become the extroverts on tour, loud and gregarious in finding a new freedom when released from the restrictive borders of normal family life. Then there are the ones who never change whatever the situation, apart from when homesickness strikes. Homesickness catches up with everybody at some stage or another.

There is still another group – the jokers with a quip for every occasion who raise the spirits when the side is down, and crack the air of tension with a word or act when the feelings are aroused. The Robin Hobbs and "Ollie" Milburns of the cricketing world are worth a place on any touring party as a mascot, irrespective of their cricketing ability. I've toured with them both, and drawn pleasure and comfort from their presence.

Every team should have a joker in the pack at home as well as abroad for there is no doubt that the demands on the cricketer have grown tremendously in recent years. I know there was more cricket 20 or so years ago when teams played 32 championship matches a season. But the pressures on the player were not as great as today, with the constant scrutiny of television, four different competitions (perhaps six for a Test player) and with prize money as well as pride at stake.

It is not just the physical and mental demands of playing cricket seven days a week but many other factors as well that have helped to increase the strain. The worst is the travelling, the dashing from one ground to another, especially the Friday evening–Monday morning roundabout routine. Motorway journeying from one hotel bed to another, grabbing meals when possible, is a strain arranged by a computer spilling out fixtures without a care for human feelings.

Some journeys are ridiculous. Cricket is no longer a pleasure when players step out on to the field, tired and worn out by travelling and lack of sleep, yet still expected to entertain.

One of the worst I have encountered was during the summer of 1974 which took us from Tunbridge Wells to Gloucester, Colwyn Bay, Moreton-in-Marsh, back to Colwyn Bay and finally to Brighton all within eight days. Some 1,400 miles in all mainly on cross-country routes filled with holiday traffic at the height of the summer, with cricket for six hours a day between trips.

By the time we had finished the Gloucester match on the Friday, washed, showered, packed, said farewell, negotiated the heavy traffic and stopped for an evening meal, it was well after midnight when we arrived at North Wales. The following evening, after a full day in the field against Glamorgan, we had to dash 200 miles to Worcester to stop overnight. Sunday morning it was on to Moreton-in-Marsh for our John Player League match against Gloucester.

That was bad enough. Getting back was worse as we had to make the journey in one go and were unable to leave Moreton-in-Marsh until after 7 p.m. It was about two in the morning before we found our North Wales hotel again, with another day's cricket only seven hours away by the time we had got to sleep. It turned out to be a wasted weekend journey for me. I caught a 48-hour bug on Saturday night and was creased up with agony by the time I arrived in Moreton-in-Marsh where a local doctor was called and told me not to play. I was not the only Sussex player to suffer but was the worst of the sick parade. It was not the most memorable weekend of my life but one I shall not easily forget. How we managed to beat Kent and Gloucestershire twice I shall never know. Sheer cussedness on our part, I suppose, plus determination to show that we could beat a system which was all against us being at our best.

That weekend was exceptional but we have had similar experiences since the growth of one-day cricket. Financially welcome as it has been, the new style of cricket has brought with it an additional burden of chasing from ground to ground as well as the need to adapt to different playing regulations and rules day after day.

This has been so demanding that I was staggered when proposals were put forward during the 1975 – 76 winter to increase the county championship from 20 to 24 matches because of the free dates available once sides have been eliminated from the Benson and Hedges Cup or the Gillette Cup.

I cannot see the logic of such an idea. The clubs will earn peanuts which will hardly be worth the extra work involved. County championship matches are not money spinners any more. In mid-week they are played before near-deserted grounds and the money taken from these extra matches will not make any noticeable difference to the balance sheet at the end of the year.

If any changes were to be made I would have thought a reduction in the number of championship matches was necessary. A cut from 20 to 16 games during the summer would produce a fairer championship, with each side playing the others once only.

The actual number of playing days would be raised from the present maximum of 60 to 64 by making the games stretch over four days instead of three. This would at least give an excuse to increase membership charges. Not that an excuse is needed in my opinion. It seems ridiculous that until recently you could obtain life membership of Sussex for only £100 yet have to pay £30 or so for a season ticket to watch Third Division football at Brighton just down the road.

There would be numerous benefits in switching championship matches to four days. Apart from the obvious one of increasing the likelihood of an outright result in games where the weather had caused a lengthy interference, it would help the groundsman, who would have to find room for only eight first-class strips instead of the present ten or the proposed twelve. It would also give him more time to prepare each wicket properly instead of trying to fit each in like a piece in a giant jig-saw as many have to do at the moment, particularly at Lord's. Four-day matches would certainly help to bring back the art of spin bowling, for spinners would have to bowl more and would also be needed to take advantage of the wickets breaking up on the last day. It might even save the leg spinner before he becomes extinct.

Many of cricket's ills in England I blame on the wickets. Most of them are a disgrace, and have helped to reduce the standard of cricket on many days, as well as to stunt the development of cricketers. They are part of the reason why England has been searching in vain for the next Dexter, May or Hutton and for bowlers of genuine pace to match the fire of Lillee, Thomson, Roberts, Holding and the rest.

Players have been complaining about the standard of wickets for a number of years but, if anything, they are getting worse. Not even county captains have been able to influence the wicket-makers, as Mike Brearley found out when he attempted to get something done about the Middlesex wickets on their rented ground at Lord's.

Mike, the Middlesex captain, in a series of conversations with the groundsman, complained about the standard of the wickets. Especially he complained about a bad one provided for an important game against Leicestershire when in the previous game (MCC v Scotland), there had been a belter of a wicket to play on. The net result of his efforts was nil for the MCC Ground Committee instructed the groundsman not to talk to him in future.

All wickets should be hard and fast at the start, offering the fast bowler an opportunity to extract pace and bounce and some true reward for his skill. Such wickets would also give the batsman a chance to stroke the ball to the boundary. With the ball coming on to the bat, timing becomes an essential quality. A correct touch should be all that is needed to get the ball away instead of the brute force batsmen often have to employ today.

Bounce, too, would give the spinner a chance to return to his true role, that of being an attacking bowler – like the genuine quickie – instead of a stock bowler with a flat and fast trajectory.

What do we find now from one county ground to another? Flat, "nothing" wickets where the ball rarely gets above stump high once the hardness has gone out of the ball after the first morning. Wickets that penalise genuine class, whether it is produced by the bowler or the batsman. Wickets where the batsman has to work hard for his runs even against medium military pace, which would be slaughtered in any other part of the world.

For years we have been promised action yet nothing has been produced except a string of reasons to say why the wickets are not as they should be. In 1975 it was blamed on the wet winter preventing the groundstaff putting down the necessary preparations. In 1976 it was blamed on the dry winter, although I would have thought this was ideal; groundsmen could have watered the square when and how they wanted in the right quantity to produce the growth they needed.

Perhaps the county organisations must take a lot of the blame. In the first place they have not offered the right wages to attract the best to the game. Secondly they should insist that wickets are up to standard and ban the widespread use of Surrey loam, which in my opinion has done more than anything to slow the wickets down.

I am willing to bet that not a county ground in England has avoided Surrey loam, which cannot be a universal panacea for all squares are different. Fielding at Lord's in 1975 I was standing on a used wicket, and with a suitable implement I could have skimmed the top half inch from that pitch like taking icing off a cake. In my opinion, that is the result of Surrey loam. Such wickets breed insecurity in batsmen, who cannot tell what the ball will do next.

Until the wickets get back to an acceptable standard England will never produce the stroke-playing batsmen, genuine fast bowlers and spinners necessary to make a good side. Most of the trouble English batsmen encounter in playing genuine pace is caused because they have limited experience of playing it. When asked to play on wickets in the West Indies and Australia, they find cricket suddenly becomes a different game, although even in these countries some wickets have lost their pace.

To say English batsmen lack courage – as has been hinted on more than one occasion in the last few years – is wrong. I know them personally, have lived with them, shared dressing rooms with them and I know many would stand up to Lillee, Holding and company if only they had the experience to give them the right technique.

When discussing my school days earlier in this book I said I was fortunate to get my early training at Christ's Hospital on wickets which were superior to the majority I came across later in the first-class game. It was a tremendous boost to my career. I was not the only fortunate one.

Look at some of England's finest stroke-making batsmen over the years. The majority of them came from a public school background, fortunate to get their early introduction to the game on good wickets. First at their public schools and later at Fenners and The Parks, the home grounds of Cambridge and Oxford Universities.

It is not surprising that English cricket was forced to turn to overseas players such as Barry Richards, Gary Sobers, Clive Lloyd, Alvin Kallicharran, Brian Davison and the rest to provide some of the lost sparkle. They all grew up in countries where good, true wickets were the rule rather than the exception; where young batsmen were taught to attack instead of how to survive at the crease.

Test match wickets have been just as bad, and that includes Lord's where it was once a joy to play. The wickets for the last half-dozen one-day finals have come under criticism, and Sussex had a bad one the last time we played there in 1973 against Gloucestershire in the Gillette final. Lord's must have received so many adverse reports in recent years I am sure it would have joined the list of grounds banned as unsuitable for first-class cricket but for the fact that it is the home of the MCC.

Equally, the Oval wickets have been a disaster in recent Tests. In the final Test against Australia in 1975 six days went by – seven including the rest day – without a result being achieved, despite the presence of Thomson and Lillee in the Australian side. The Test wickets at Edgbaston and Trent Bridge have been little better. Yet Test matches are supposed to be the show-pieces of the summer, the settings for all that is best in the game. The players should have the best of conditions. Imagine the outcry from the contestants if the World Professional Snooker Championship were played on a table with a wrinkled cloth.

It is a tragedy because players' livings often depend on the conditions under which they play. If we fail to do our job properly then we are out. We lose money if we are dropped from the Test side, and even more if left out of the county team. Yet success is a yardstick that does not apply to many other people employed in various other capacities in the game, whether they are the people who make the decisions or those who are forced to carry them out. Their inefficiency goes unpunished. Once again it is the unfortunate player who suffers.

The question of finding the right people to fill the various roles is applicable to Test selectors. They are selected themselves from a list of candidates put forward by the county clubs. Too often county clubs nominate people to reward them for long service rather than choose them for their qualities as potential selectors.

It became so bad that a special sub-committee of the TCCB Cricket Committee was formed to try to find suitable candidates to stand as Test selectors, and persuade them to devote time to the job. Happily, it has led to Ken Barrington and Charlie Elliot coming on to the selection panel, two men with the ideal qualifications.

It is still not right as Graham Gooch discovered on his Test debut against the Australians at Edgbaston in 1975. Sir Leonard Hutton was chatting to him and asked: "Have you played against the Australians before?" An innocent enough question on the surface. Yet remarkable coming from a selector, considering the young Essex batsman had gained his opportunity largely as a result of two innings for the MCC against the Australians at Lord's less than a fortnight earlier.

On another occasion I happened to hear someone ask Sir Leonard how he managed to fit in all his selectorial duties and was astonished to hear him reply: "I read the newspapers and I have my contacts up and down the country." Surely it is no way to select a Test side on what other people say, when careers are at stake. It is exactly this off-hand attitude towards players that I feel so strongly about.

Glancing back through these pages I suppose I have been critical, in the main, of the game that has enabled me to go all over the world and earn a living. People will no doubt say that I am ungrateful. Quite the reverse, although, with the experiences I've had and the need to set the record straight by giving my version for the first time on many of them, I've had to single out some of the more unfortunate aspects.

I believe cricket to be the finest game there is to play. A game embracing the individual challenge of one against one inside the framework of a team game where eleven men are against eleven, each with his own specific role to play, but always mindful of the interests of the other ten he plays with and for.

Arthur Milton, the former Arsenal footballer and Gloucestershire batsman who represented his country at both sports, was once asked why he was carrying on for another season at an age when many men have long since cast off their boots. He replied: "Apart from the personal satisfaction I obtain from playing, I don't know of any other way of life where I could have found such friendship and comradeship as I have in cricket." I know exactly how he feels.

Ask the other cricketers who play professional football which game they prefer and I am willing to bet that the summer game would get the vote. It would be the priority sport on their list if the wages could approach those they earn during the nine months of the winter.

It is because I care for cricket and want to see it prosper and be able to offer a decent wage, because I wish to see its future secure, its horizens widen, its appeal spread, that I have been critical during the previous pages. I hope that some of the wrongs can be put right, some of the prejudices disappear and that management and players can come closer together until they work as one.

Cricket is such a fine game that I want it to stay around so that many other people in the far distant future can share the enjoyment I have derived from being part of it. I have no regrets at being drawn into its clutches to fulfil that childhood dream of so many years ago.

The Trials of Cricketers

Overseas Umpires: A Cape Town umpire called 'no ball' as I was going past him into my delivery stride. Apologising profusely, he said: "It just slipped out."

Pay: Vanburn Holder would have received more basic pay by playing for Worcestershire in 1976 than he received by being in the West Indies tour party.

Selectors: Test selector at Canterbury in 1974: "Snowey sprayed it around in his early spell". I had two wickets for about five runs. Test selector to Bob Willis as Phil Edmonds, to whom he had been chatting, went out to bat at Lord's: "Who was that man I've been talking to?"

Food: At the Trent Bridge Test in 1976 it was diabolical. At lunch, cheese and biscuits weren't allowed to those who had a sweet.

Dress: England sweaters are renewed after eight years (it used to be ten). I was told to buy a new Prudential England sweater in 1975 because I gave my original one to Dennis Lillee two years earlier.

Committee men: Kent committee man overheard outside the Lord's Tavern: "He's waiting for a benefit, but he's not getting one. He wants more money but we're not giving it to him."

Sussex committee man: "It's a pity all this Benson and Hedges money goes to the players."

. . . and finally a Sussex committee man to me: "I wouldn't like to see the game change in my life-time".

Poems

Publisher's Note

John Snow's first collection of poems, *Contrasts*, was published in 1971 by Fuller d'Arch Smith Limited, London. A second volume of poetry, *Moments and Thoughts*, was published in 1973 by Kaye and Ward Limited, London, in association with Michael de Hartington.

Some of the poems have cricketing themes and relate to events and experiences already described in this book. Others capture thoughts and impressions unconnected with cricket. All are reprinted on the following pages.

On Being Dropped

Standing
on a still summer's day,
eye watching swallows
earth-hugging
insect-chasing way,
wondering what to do,
knowing that it always happens
and now it's happened to you.
What not again? Yes.
Feeling like laughing at the fable
yet not being able
because you have no middle
and life waits watching behind
having given you the casual twiddle.
Yet as your world revolved
it spun you through a wider sky,
opened further open eye,
it's a game.
So come on, who's king of the castle
now I'm the dirty rascal,
standing,
on a still summer's day
eye watching swallows
insect-chasing way.

I Stand Watching Time Pointing

Still, like the silence of death I stand
watching time pointing
its frail clawed warty hand
and asking:
What have you done?
Turning I look for things to take and show
then realise they all vanished long ago.

Len Bates – Cricketer and Coach

You are gone now
just as in my elder youth
my first dreams are gone;
but, as with them, still
the headstone weathers on.

Young I was
yet to your wrinkled hawkish eye bountiful
and so I was garnered with farmer's care
to the barn kept ever empty waiting;
but now the years have wandered
and enwrapped in the curtain of time
they have fallen in a strangling tangle
and been buried in life's quick-lime.

Gone;
but words still forming
speak of what you say.
Gone;
but something remaining
is passed to the coming day;
Mr Bates.

Bahawalpur Ground

Behind the limpid dust-clothed trees
the pointed tower,
Moulvi waiting,
stands faded red against the blue.
Above a cheel, eying wheeling,
also views the sunbaked ground,
sees standing people kameez clad
and women burqa'd seated,
ochre-blue-red canopied,
shaded from sun's prying too.
Charred afternoon.

Pakistan Troubles – Lahore

A tree, vulture-topped, standing
shading a policeman, lathi-armed, waiting
by barbed wire sown on the road
for a car to pass with its worried load.

Frustration

The wheel which turns
is turning much faster than before
while hands that claw the wall
wear down their nails still more.
On the treadmill rolls
as the body mindless bowls
down paths
and the wheel which turns
is turning much faster than before.

Road to Lyallpur

What if eternal darkness slapped your face
or a noseless man touched your hand,
would the puking rise
from where it lies,
would you feel small,
a part of the damned?
Can you never see,
can you never feel
what to some poor bastard
is so very very real?

Lord's Test

Tomorrow starts the night before
lying looking through the blackness
wondering about the hidden day
'til falling forward trackless
unknowing down the slope,
you're there sitting in it,
you and hope.
Eyes forage and find it's real
together with the growing tugging
that you feel in your stomach
as morning spreads like a ripple
from your movement towards the ground,
where gates opening, welcome,
then close in daylong vice-embrace
leaving time to sneak in round.

Eventually, after dressing-room chaos of
body and mind,
the moment comes . . .
down,
past longroom critics
who ever change, thistledown's way,
in the breeze
summer day over summer's day,
to sudden silence of your tread
on grass where lie, not dead
but shining reclining,
the deeds of many hallowed.

Time to admire the wealth of the hour
and on its virgin page,
place a memoir of your passing life
while umpire's back is turned,
beneath a sun that has spun
ever brighter on its path.

Later, spiritlike,
while Father Time above the northern stand
eyes the breeze,
you move aside
and see a body flailing,
bowl a ball swinging

along its way, batsman playing,
and remember, outside the wall
people weave their webs of life
with you on the lattice day
which is everyone's,
yet is an age within an age,
a life within a life,
as minutes pass awestruck
up to lunch and over.

On you toil again
across the width of the afternoon,
with scoreboards catching all
like fishmongers' wives
and showing on their faces
what lies behind their eyes.
Even clouds pry, small in blue above,
to see with you on Tavern balcony
chairs half tulip-cupped
red-yellow blazing
sunfired;
unlike flats beyond, which dull,
sentry stiff forward stare,
and glassy eyed, rejecting ray,
miss the colours of people sitting, watching, thinking,
until tea, as Nursery trees wave.

Now, though the day relaxes,
limbs and brain tighten,
unlike those that lighten
in the Tavern and birdsnest boxes;
Yet reality crystallises
and the press-box creaking, stretching,
fidgeting, vulture-like waits
with the sound of sharpening carbon claws
for the fresh caress of play.
Time drags itself past,
and evening forewarns spreading its musk
in the approaching cloud of dusk,
till at last
the bowler flails once more,
a final twitch for the dying day.
Then leaving bruised pitch to sleep,
stumps are drawn,

and dazed, amazed it's over,
you hold ragged muscles together
long enough to climb the stairs
and reach a bath
before you collapse, to let its warmth
smooth and soothe
and laugh an aching laugh.

Dacca Morning, 1969

The sun rising eastwards
bleaches the night,
shining pierces
kameez's of white,
shows standing camels'
lofty gaze at the haze
of a day that waits
with pitiful beggars'
empty stare.
Later the hour is full
of the brown of earth,
of the lack of laughter
and casual mirth,
for the child is stillborn
in the heat of the day
and there is nothing to chase
tomorrow away.

Skip the world
like a pebble the flatness of a pond
watch ripples circle
each touch and spread,
skip on,
skip lower,
till the force is gone,
then drop
and drop
through the water,
the clear clear water.

Have You Been to Pitchpartoo?

Have you been to Pitchpartoo and Porepu
or places such as these
where emerald palms wave frayed arms
on sands by tropical seas;
where cobalt rollers come to rest,
silver crests 'neath a smiling sun,
where nobody worries shouts or hurries
and everything is cheerfully done;
where life is life
not a bitchy strife
being fought in a gathering gloom
with everything handled and hopelessly tangled
like threads on a drunkard's loom?
If you have not, review your lot
fly where dawn tints the eastern sky
then as you free the hook and turn to look
you will see with a jewel for an eye.

The Hand is Taken

The hand stretched is taken
and the room,
caressed with music, thoughts,
and moments of writers' past,
surrenders,
for canopied, spotlit,
and splashed gold with clapping also
the singer king holds rich court
aided by his jester band.
Dais throned
microphone orbed,
he in his time spreads emotional peace and war
ruling as others faded likewise did before.

Looking at the Present

Looking at the present
Lying weighty in her hands she asked,
"Why didn't you do that earlier?"
to which I replied,
"Would it have MADE a difference?
Would it have made MUCH difference?
Would it have made THAT MUCH difference?
Out here and inside?"

"Everyone needs some sign of love," she murmured
raising her eyes to me.
"Some people know no deserts; others know no sea,
everyone needs to be taken and shown
things that can really be."

"I merely judged what I could honestly judge
and did what I could honestly do
while standing watching the face of time
hiding in the shadow of you.
Did I do wrong to look so much
when following a wandering road?
What would you say if I told you today
tomorrow is the heaviest load?"

"Talk and talk like that if you will
but would you be right?" she asked.
"What is the force that makes you think
tomorrow is today's task?"

"All right, no point, I'd better go
for what is there left to say?
You are not with me so we'd never see
that which we both should know.
Maybe the schemes and the prodigal dreams
are best left in the sleeper's bed.
Maybe the oughts and countless thoughts
best left in the thinker's head.
Yet as I leave light pale bled
perhaps you'd consider this
that a door is opened and a door is closed
and the living are also the dead."

October – Bognor Beach

Rocks, blackened roots, protrude
from the receding gum of sea
while the head of the pier stands ghostly separate
from the body where it really should be
and people, black crabs scuttling, claw
reflecting sheen of sand
for wormbait to hook later
with fisherman's numbed gnarled hand.
Bognor beach on gathering October night
winked at by Owers ever-brightening light
a cyclops eye in scenes clouding forehead
and the end of a day too quickly read.

See the Saffron Sunlight

See the saffron sunlight
falling softly on her hair
watch the silken strands
play innocently with the air,
follow the willowy movements
as she wanders through the grass
and know now quietly pondering
love's softly come to pass.

The face is not perfect
that houses those hazel eyes
the lips are no different,
like all, they've told their lies,
yet we understand each other
and can honestly declare
we have something good to add
something we both can share.

Brighton Seafront – September

The black velvet dome of jailer night
confines a hazy blaze of seafront light
and clamps vision's neck
but misses sea pressing flat
stealthily sliding under to touch
then turn again for places that
mysteriously it came from.
Standing, feeling and listening
only seafront rail restrains,
stops you running down shingle bank
after water's siren call
that tugging through stillness dreamy warm
and casting languid spell
makes eastern sights and tropical nights
seem strangely close at hand
when in fact they only beckon
in some far-off land.

The Clock Ricochets

The clock ricochets in its shell,
the rain has stopped
and in the velvet night
thoughts of you well.
Away out there a weary car clambers up the road
and voices float as music wandering
helps neighbours free the load.
Here four-walled softly nestled,
carried soundless through the labyrinth
I wonder where you are
and of what I can be certain,
when day reveals the scene
the other side of night's curtain.

Being a Child of Life

Being a child of life
I am eternally young
even though my time is long
and many a different song is sung,
while the age of the earth bears witness
together with the stupidity of man
to the cast-eyed vision
of you and I since we began.
It's not another world you know
just another country
not somewhere new to go
just another side of man to see.
A mind is wide
and should be free
to grow round in the crystal ball
that is eternity.

Let Me Pillar Myself

Let me pillar myself
with the gods
for they can speak
when I am dumb.

The sea and shingle
quietly whisper,
breeze drifts gently on
while the bird that's singing
takes to winging
and soon is gone.

Anne

Tomorrow is already here
in the evening of today
for though the path is not lit
I'm moving on my way.

The presence which is now
cannot, unlike the mind,
be carried to tomorrow's
richer fields you'll find.

So the kiss is left,
the touch withheld undone
for the tears you cry will dry
in tomorrow's warmer sun.

The Willow

Now the willow, hair hang-downing,
bows the stream a sad farewell
as it goes on yet careering
down beyond that shady dell.

There in that cool quiet surrounding
all of life does compassed lie
while birth, but slow, spreads joy abounding
death so fast rips breath awry.

Yet the waters bound on yonder,
joyfully they leap away,
leaving stones so cold and sombre
in the warmth and light of day.

So the willow's tears unending
damp the ground but every day
while green hair droops and deep in shadow
hides the face of truth for ay.

Autumn

The silk touch
of the hand
that washes the day with rain
soothes the mind,
while gold drops of tears
slipping warm from the trees
are shed as fears,
till the serenity of the look
in the calm eye of evening
transfixes.

From a Window

Rain softly falling
slips to the ground.
Spider slow weaving
round and around.
Mere droplet laden
the widening web
as yet untainted,
clear, holds no dread.

Hand eager catches
drops as they fall.
Eye quietly watches
but cannot see all.
Fingers close tightly;
they still slip away
down, always moving,
come what may.

Now the fly circling
is caught web-bound
while rain softly falling
slips to the ground.

You, and me

Go on little one and play your games;
let the sun circle you in the warmth of day,
for when it descends in the evening mist
and your wishes have all been wished,
then to yourself you've your confession to say.

Go When You Go

Go, when you go,
with me
for my thoughts you carry
sewn in your tread;
then when you've gone
and the empty day gets old
at least I am left with something warm to hold.

Silver Winged

Silver winged and sun eye watched,
southward racing, cylinder held
and false air fed
I slide over ground helpless
where you four wheeled previous sped.

I'm time stamped and future weighted
going forward, sitting back
and moving not
while shepherding thoughts your way
running shoeless over the unfenced plot.

Au Revoir

The day fleeing from the evening
waves honeyed thoughts of you
before its warm receding face
but misguided falls into
advancing arms of night's octopus embrace.
Lengthening like my meditation
shadows spread with the passing time,
then merge in gentle weddings
form one family eternal and sublime.

Watching so and turning round
each moment's passing form
searching slow the mental loft,
looking for life's downy nape,
gently resting in safe harbour
after rounding storm-swept cape.

Question

What are my dreams
a life that is unseen?
What is tomorrow then
but a dream?
If I said I loved you
would the heavens open wide,
would that swirling whirling churning feeling
burst inside,
then when that had settled to a gentle sway,
could my touch lie on your cheek
in the eye of day?

When You See

When you see,
then close your eyes,
and what do you see?

In the Blackness of a Coffee Cup

In the blackness of a coffee cup
that was laid before us
eternity rolled its way
shadowed by Venus and Mars
to leave us bare in nonentity.
But still the fact was there
in reflection;
still the thought was there
on reflection. Reflection.

Now the sky streaming blood
dips to bathe
its bullet wound
in the flat gelid water
while seagulls scream in anguish;
but in bending lower
the vermilion stain,
irretrievably is spread
the bloody circle
is submerged
and the day dying
collapses into the slate grey sea.

Mole black and soft
the night built its hills upon us
till engulfed
we were buried in its ethereal tomb
and time was lost
like honeysuckle scent on a summer breeze.

Satin Silk Summer Air

Satin silk summer air
now wrapped in night's velvet grasp
and weighing heavy in its hand,
is anxious to be free.
Waiting you and I
breathless, sense the moment
and add our watching heat
to the oppressive struggle.
A sylph wind joins us
and murmurs at the villain night
yet cannot change its will
and nor can we
for only the wayward sun
may release for good or ill.

City Pilgrim

You rattle down the track
seabound
like a ship down a slipway
toward the Sound and waiting freedom
to be known
in its circle of the world:
then leaving train at cluttered station
like ship leaves cluttered land
you make a way to your destination
of that verging golden strand
to stand on the edge of freshness
by the curling rolling waves
with arms outstretched to feel the space
that a city pilgrim craves.

Now at the Moment

Now at the moment
when I want to hear you,
locked in torment,
reaching to be near you,
I curse the distance
that hell bent
knowing will not relent.

Butterfly leaving petal
in the day of its life,
scythe cutting nettle
clean as sounding fife
like a blues singer sorrowfully
singing his song
with these thoughts passing
from where I would belong.

Ferris wheel turned
and the base rearrived,
shipwrecked sailor mourned
near one that has survived,
uncut pages parted
splitting what was one,
a tune that is ending
note dying, slipping, gone.

Wind chasing cloud
in a field high above
river babbling loud
giggling out its love,
like a lark still rising
from the field where it lay
I'm a blues singer smiling
singing to the day.

Index